BETJEMAN'S LONDON

EDITED BY
Pennie Denton

JOHN MURRAY

For
R C Player

Designed by Mike Head

© This selection the Literary Executors of John Betjeman 1988
© Preface and footnotes Pennie Denton 1988
First published 1988
by John Murray (Publishers) Ltd
50 Albemarle Street, London, W1X 4BD

Printed and bound in Great Britain
by Butler and Tanner Ltd, Frome.

British Library Cataloguing in Publication Data

Betjeman, John, *1906–1984*
  Betjeman's London.
  I. Title   II. Denton, Pennie
  828'.91208
  ISBN 0-7195-4494-7

Contents

Preface

John Betjeman was born in London and lived there, in Highgate, the City and Chelsea, for most of his life. In his poems, in his writings for newspapers and magazines, radio and television, in letters to *The Times* and in well-publicised campaigns, he celebrated London and fought to save it from 'The Planster's Vision'.

While he was still a baby his parents moved from Parliament Hill Mansions, Lissenden Gardens up the hill, and social scale, to 31, West Hill, Highgate where he grew up 'safe in a world of trains and buttered toast'. His childhood security was shattered, however, first by a sadistic nursery-maid and then, when he was eleven, by the family move to Chelsea:

> What is it first breeds insecurity?
> Perhaps a change of house? I missed the climb
> By garden walls and fences where a stick,
> Dragged in the palings, clattered to my steps.
> I missed the smell of trodden leaves and grass,
> Millfield and Merton Lanes and sheep-worn tracks
> Under the hawthorns west of Highgate Ponds.

John Betjeman's ability to evoke his childhood landscape in this passage from his autobiography *Summoned by Bells*, is characteristic; memories and a sense of place pervade his poems whether they are about bygone Middlesex or churches or railway stations. Most of the poems here are in his *Collected Poems*; 'Chelsea 1977' and 'St Mary Magdalen, Old Fish Street Hill' come from *Uncollected Poems*. A few others were written to draw attention to the possible destruction of a building and have only appeared as pamphlets or in newspapers. Even in ceremonial poems, like that written for the Lord Mayor of London's March and printed in *The Times*, he continued to campaign, insisting that this verse should not be omitted:

> The many-steepled sky
> Which made our City fair,
> Buried in buildings high
> Is now no longer there.

It is hardly surprising that Philip Larkin felt that 'at Betjeman's heart is not poetry but architecture – or, if the concepts are allowed, a poetry that embraces architecture and an architecture that embraces poetry.'

In a lecture delivered in 1937, and published two years later as 'Antiquarian Prejudice', John Betjeman said, 'Architecture means not a house, or a single building or a Church, or Sir Herbert Baker, or the glass at Chartres, but your surroundings; not a town or a street but our whole overpopulated island.' He wanted not just to save individual buildings but to fight to maintain the human scale in our towns and cities; he knew from his own experience how insecure people can feel when their surroundings are changed. His first conservation campaign began while he was working at *The Architectural Review* in the 1930s with an article on the threat to Rennie's masterpiece, Waterloo Bridge, and the first of over seventy campaigning letters to *The Times*. Waterloo Bridge was not saved and neither was the Euston Arch which he first wrote about in 1933 and was still writing about in 1963 when it was finally demolished. In the course of the battle to save Euston Arch the Victorian Society was formed with John Betjeman as a founder member. It may seem strange now but in the 1950s most people considered anything Victorian hideously ugly and the gradual change in attitude must, in part, have been brought about by John Betjeman. Subsequent campaigns often triumphed just because he supported them. When he died in 1984 *The Times* wrote, 'his enthusiasm made him perhaps the most influential conservationist of his time' and it is heartening that some of the buildings he wrote about in the 1950s, notably the Criterion Theatre and Brasserie and the churches of St Saviour, Aberdeen Park and St Mary-le-Strand, have recently been restored.

In the 1950s John Betjeman, who since his marriage to Penelope Chetwode in 1933 had lived in the country, began to spend more time at his London base at 43, Cloth Fair in the City. From 1954 to 1958 he wrote a weekly column in *The Spectator* called 'City and Suburban' in which he drew attention to the horrors of sodium lights and concrete lamp posts, the siting of pylons and nuclear power stations and airports, ribbon development and the destruction of country houses and worthwhile buildings in London to make way for 'the new packing-cases, miscalled towers'. His 'Men and Buildings' articles in *The Daily Telegraph*, which appeared between 1959 and 1964, examined architectural issues in greater depth as well as continuing earlier campaigns. In 1977 he reluctantly left the City, forced out by the noise and traffic, and moved to 29, Radnor Walk, Chelsea, where he lived for the rest of his life.

Those familiar with John Betjeman's writings will not be surprised to find a good deal on churches and railways in this book, but they may be surprised to find him wandering in parks, visiting the Isle of Dogs and rhapsodising about the attractions of London airport. It is interesting, too, to find him anticipating recent developments by suggesting that Covent Garden would make a charming shopping arcade and dockland's warehouses delightful flats. The best possible companion on a walk around London, he opened the eyes of friends, acquaintances and then television audiences to unexpected corners, unseen decoration and unrealised beauty. His erudition, especially on all aspects of architecture, his natural talent as a raconteur and his humour, turned the smallest expedition into a magical tour illuminating not only the surroundings but man's ability to create and destroy, his genius and his fallibility, his propensity for happiness and sadness. John Betjeman's book *Vintage London* was published during the war when petrol was rationed and destruction was by enemy action rather than developers, but his introduction might well be borrowed for this: 'So this book is in the nature of an escape. Here and there it is possible to rediscover old London, now that the petrol fumes have died away and big business turned its attention away from bricks and fields. It is not my intention to provide a guide but an escape.'

PENNIE DENTON
November 1987

Acknowledgements

My particular thanks are due to: the Executors of John Betjeman's Estate, John Grey Murray, Edward Bawden, the BBC Written Archives Centre at Caversham, Dennis Edwards, J. P. Foster – Surveyor of the Fabric at Westminster Abbey, John Gay, Mrs Gwnydd Gosling of the Highgate Literary and Scientific Institution, the photographic and print libraries at the Greater London Record Office, Roger Hudson, Ralph Hyde at the Guildhall Library, Sir Denys Lasdun, John Piper, and Swiss Cottage Local History Library.

Picture Acknowledgements

Walter Thornbury, *Old and New London* (n.d.) frontispiece, 163; the late Sir Osbert Lancaster 4, 20, 48/49, 57; BBC Hulton Picture Library 8, 63, 122, 159; Greater London Record Office (maps and prints) 10, 17, 42, 50, 55, 58, 66, 71, 92, 95, 99, 100, 124, 146, 148/149, 151, 155, 158, 170, 178, 180, 182; *Cornhill Magazine* (1862) 13; T. H. Shepherd, *Metropolitan Improvements* (1828) 14; John Gay 15, 18, 22, 24, 34, 60, 108, 128, 133, 160, 164, 186; Jonathan Stedall 21; London Transport Museum 27; London Borough of Camden Local History Library 32; Curtis Brown Ltd for the late Ernest Shepard's surrounds from *Punch* 36, 51, 121; Bernard Alfieri 40; *Life Magazine* (Mark Kaufmann) 41, 52; John Piper 44/45; BBC Enterprises 72, 96, 175; *The Builder* (6/10/1888) 68, (11/12/1886) 136; Gavin Stamp 70; The editor of *Punch* 73, 74, 75; C. R. L. Coles 76; *Sunday Telegraph* Colour Magazine (Bill Brandt) 80, 82; London Borough of Ealing Local History Library 84; *Country Life* 87; Edward Bawden 103, 107, 110, 112, 115, 116; Westminster City Archives 119; E. R. Robson, *School Architecture* (1874) 125; Royal Commission on Historical Monuments 127; *Picturesque London* (n.d.) 134; *Ballet* (11/51) 138; London Borough of Hackney Archives Dept 142, 176; Camera Press 147; London Borough of Islington Libraries Dept 168; Southwark Local Studies Library 183; Alex McCarren 184.

INTRODUCING LONDON

I suppose nearly everything I have written this
week can be called 'nostalgic'. It is a scientific
word for 'sentimental' and sounds like a form of
catarrh . . . I regard 'nostalgic' as a term of praise,
myself, for it implies reverence and a sense of the
past and awareness of, though not necessarily a
slavery to, tradition.

SPECTATOR. 29 OCTOBER 1954

Meditation on a Constable Picture

Go back in your mind to that Middlesex height
Whence Constable painted the breeze and the light
As down out of Hampstead descended the chaise
To the wide-spreading valley, half-hidden in haze:

The slums of St. Giles, St. Mary'bone's farms,
And Chelsea's and Battersea's riverside charms,
The palace of Westminster, towers of the Abbey
And Mayfair so elegant, Soho so shabby,

The mansions where lilac hangs over brown brick,
The ceilings whose plaster is floral and thick,
The new stucco terraces facing the park,
The odorous alleyways, narrow and dark,

The hay barges sailing, the watermen rowing
On a Thames unembanked which was wide and slow-flowing,
The street-cries rebounding from pavements and walls
And, steeple-surrounded, the dome of St. Paul's.

Vintage London

From the book of that title. 1942

To discover London you must know how London grew. It consists of three towns little more than a penny bus fare apart, Southwark, London and Westminster. These towns have absorbed villages and whole counties, but they still retain their individuality as do many of the villages lost in the forest of building.

I put Southwark first because it is most likely that it was a Roman settlement before London. Though it is oldest, it is the dimmest of the three towns and it lost its independence in 1461 when the City absorbed it. It has returned members to Parliament since 1296. Today the collection of wharfs about London Bridge, the stumpy tower of Southwark Cathedral Church, the uneven Borough High Street and market wedged in among railway viaducts, one galleried inn *The George*, a hospital, an eighteenth-century church turned chapter house, are all that remains to remind us of the town from which Chaucer's pilgrims set out for Canterbury.

London, the next town, a City with a Lord Mayor, Aldermen and Councillors, is the most important of the three. It is about one square mile in area and an ingenious writer, Sir Lawrence Gomme, has shown how its Roman origin has survived until today. The main streets cross at right angles in Roman fashion, and it is worth noting that the chief roads into London and Southwark are nearly all of Roman origin: Watling Street, Old Kent Road, Portsmouth Road, the roads to Silchester and Colchester. London Wall is still the Roman wall. London stone, a worn piece of limestone let into the wall of St Swithin's church opposite Cannon Street Station, is of Roman origin and still revered. St Paul's is built on the site of a Roman temple to Diana, Leadenhall market was a public meeting place in Roman times. Certainly London citizens have retained strong individuality and privileges. They used the Barons for getting rid of the King's privileges, they used the Guilds of Craftsmen for removing the Barons, they used Parliamentary Acts for curtailing the power of the Guilds, finally they built over the numerous priories and friaries which, until the Reformation, occupied one third of the area of the City. From then on Christianity and commerce parted for good.

First the City was a fortified, walled collection of stone buildings dominated by the Norman Tower. Later it became less fortified, houses were built outside the walls, palaces for the nobility along the banks of the Thames to the island of Westminster. The Savoy Hotel takes its name from the house of the Earls of Savoy built in 1245. Houses for artisans and craftsmen who were not citizens of London and members of the jealous guilds grew up in East London. St Paul's increased in size until it was the biggest cathedral in Europe and from its eminence dominated the city.

Westminster, the third town, grew round the Abbey built on an island in the Thames marshes by Edward the Confessor, who finished it in 1065. The present building was started by Henry III on the site of the Confessor's church, which had been the largest church in Northern Europe. From Edward's day until the present Westminster has been the Royal town. Kings have lived at Westminster Palace, Whitehall Palace, St James's Palace, Buckingham Palace, all in the neighbourhood of the Abbey. Westminster has always kept aloof from the City and to this day, when the King drives to the City, the Mayor comes to the Temple Bar to meet him. A drunk person may puzzle the police by creating a disturbance at the site of the Temple Bar in Fleet Street, where the City and Westminster meet. The City Police will prefer that the Metropolitan Police arrest him, the Metropolitan Police would rather leave him to the City.

Imagine a distant view of the three towns in Henry VI's time: a walled city with a forest of church towers rising above the walls, white above the marshes of the Thames, a bridge with many irregular arches and supporting houses and chapels, crossing to Southwark which is little more than a large village. A few houses along the wide shallow banks of the Thames and in the distance the city of Westminster, the Abbey rising white above the palaces.

These three, not unusual, medieval cities were to become the centre of the world's trade and the largest capital in the world. Edward IV, by no means as incompetent as history books tell us, became a wool merchant when he was King in the late fifteenth century and exported to Flanders. The Netherlands were then the central trading places of Northern Europe, Antwerp the most prosperous city. In Queen Elizabeth's reign Antwerp was sacked by the Duke of Alva and London got its trade. From her reign until today London has increased without a check.

But a love of private property, which grew up among laymen after the break-up of Christendom, hindered any planned development. Inigo Jones laid out wide squares, Lincolns Inn Fields (1618) and Covent Garden (1631). But the squares alone remain. No wide road leads to them. Men clung to their property. In 1666 London was burnt to the ground, the bricks powdered, the timber-framed buildings were charred and useless. Sir Christopher Wren laid out a plan for the whole city, with wide streets and economically used space. Private property put a stop to his plan and all he rebuilt was St Paul's and numerous city churches and a few secular buildings.

Throughout the seventeenth century London spread towards Westminster in a haphazard fashion. Fearful slums, little houses, dark alleys, no trees, no light; the city was half dwelling houses and half offices: and the dwellings spread over Southwark and Spitalfields and Whitechapel, and along the river below London Bridge among the docks, for no large vessels could navigate old London Bridge.

In the Age of Reason, the eighteenth century, London began to spread in better order. Until 1700 it was impossible for any one living in London to be more than a mile from the open country. By 1800 the distance had been doubled, but most of the walk to the country was through straight and seemly streets of tall houses, the earlier ones distinguished by brownish-red bricks, thick window bars, square-headed front doors, with carved wood (Queen Anne's Gate), the later ones by yellow-black brick (Bloomsbury, Harley Street, Wimpole Street), windows with thin glazing bars, window openings decreasing in size from the ground or first floor upwards, round-headed front doors with fanlights of lead in various patterns to admit light into the hall.

Cavendish Square (1717) started the fashion for ample squares and the Berkeley estate and the Grosvenor estate laid out squares and streets leading to them. The Portman estate followed. The families which owned land in West London soon grew rich. In 1768 the Adam Brothers, Scottish architects with a genius for speculative building, raised the Adelphi (demolished in 1938) on the North Bank of the Thames by Charing Cross, and in 1804 an architect in the Adam manner, Thomas Leverton, laid out Bedford Square. At this time too Leverton laid out Harley Street and Wimpole Street, those regular, weary rows where the Doctors wait to foretell death as politely as possible.

'Belgravia out of doors': fashionable mid-Victorian London

What cheerfulness and civic splendour London has left, what sense of planning in any grand manner that we can find in the main streets of the West End is due to John Nash the architect and his patron the Prince Regent (George IV). Nash conceived, early in the last century, the idea of a street which was to lead from Westminster to the waterless clay pasturage now known as Regent's Park, a street that was to cut through houses and join a marsh with a desert. This street, the Regent's Street, now rebuilt in a poor so-called classic style in greying dreary stone and far too high for the width of the roadway, cut off the unsavoury neighbourhood of Soho from the gentility of Hanover Square. It was diversified by a Circus at the end of Piccadilly and at Oxford Street, the road along which criminals went from the Old Bailey on their way to execution at Tyburn by the Marble Arch. From Oxford Street it joined Portland Place, a wide area terminated by the house of an obdurate Northamptonshire Baronet called Langham (the BBC's Langham building is the site of his residence), designed by the Adam Brothers. Nash built a church to break the curve he was forced to make to reach Portland Place. Beyond Portland Place, Nash built his loveliest surviving work, Park Crescent, which opened out into the pasturage. Here he planned a sort of garden city, Greek Villas to be set about in their own grounds and the whole area surrounded by terraces. Behind the Terraces, on the East side, came the Regent's Canal and alongside this he planned streets of small houses for workers in an area, now almost demolished, called Portland Town. His entire scheme was never

Drawn by Tho. H. Shepherd.   Engraved by J. Redaway

PARK CRESCENT.

Carlton House Terrace

completed and the unbuilt-on land became a public space called Regent's Park.

When George IV came to the Throne he employed Nash to build him a Palace on the site of Buckingham House (the central part, which faces down the Mall, is by Sir Aston Webb and was built in this century). Nash had the marsh between Buckingham House and Westminster laid out as a park. He designed, with his assistant James Pennethorne, Carlton House Terrace connected by a wide street with Piccadilly Circus. He also cleared the space in front of the church of St Martin's-in-the-Fields (1722–6, architect James Gibbs) and planned Trafalgar Square which was to connect with a huge square in Bloomsbury, one side of which was to be the British Museum (1823–47, architect Sir Robert Smirke).

[15]

Nash left the designing of most of the individual terraces and houses in his scheme of London improvements to brother architects: he insisted on a stucco facing to the big thoroughfares – that stucco whose pale yellow still brightens many London streets, and takes its colour from the trunks of plane trees when the bark has peeled away. Nash died in debt and in disgrace for the muddle over his designs for Buckingham Palace.

> Augustus at Rome was for building renowned
> And of marble he left what of brick he had found;
> But is not our Nash, too, a very great master?
> He finds us all brick and he leaves us all plaster.

Now that it is too late, we have come to realise that Nash was genuinely a great master, and one who knew what was the best material for building in London and where to put the streets, the houses and the trees.

Stucco streets in a classic style were built in Belgravia in the thirties, in St John's Wood (separate villas in Swiss, Gothic, Grecian and Roman styles), at Paddington in the late forties, at Pimlico in the fifties, in South Kensington in the sixties; and cheaper houses were being built in a simple classic style all over the gentle hills rising from the Thames basin – to the South at Kennington, Beulah Hill and Norwood, to the North in Islington, Hackney, Camden Town, Kentish Town, Highbury and Holloway. The market gardens and the tea gardens, the country walks that Keats had known were going down to brick. Plough was a rare sight round London now. It was all dairy farms and market gardening. Only here and there a big house stood among the encroaching streets, behind its high garden wall and its shut stable and main entrances.

A multiplicity of style succeeds the classic of Nash and his followers. By the eighteen-seventies, jerry-builders in the outer suburbs were joining what once were villages to the outlying stucco estates, with two or three storey bow-windowed villas in the Venetian gothic style – squeaking iron gates, tiles up the garden path, stone-carved capitals to the parlour window, a privet hedge behind the iron railing, bright ridge tiles and here and there the tall prickly steeple of a Gothic Revival church. Architects had become professional men and were no longer artists, and builders had set up on their own account. Neither were out to make cities, both were out to make money. The result of their work is seen all over the inner ring of outer London – Gospel Oak, Barnsbury, Finsbury Park, Wood Green, Tottenham, East Ham, New Cross, Penge, Battersea, Fulham, Willesden, Acton to name a few. It has a sinister grey and red beauty which we will one day find in the modern suburb.

There was no stinting of decoration, no lack of conviction, among these later Victorian builders; their finest achievement is the Catholic Apostolic Cathedral in Gordon Square, Bloomsbury (1855); their most ambitious

The Holborn Restaurant in 1935

effort the St Pancras Hotel and Station (1865); their wildest extravaganza the interior of the Holborn restaurant;* their largest incursion into conscious stylism, the red acreage of Willet-land,† that area of Dutch-style houses in red brick around Cadogan Square and Sloane Square, a style which was to be the inspiration for many a corbelled, balconied, stone-dressed, french-windowed block of solid pre-war flats, known in their luxurious days as 'mansions'.

As for any plan for London, that was long forgotten. Railways were allowed to ramble where they liked right into the heart of the City. Fields were filled with as many houses as could be built to the acre allowing for the garden which the new suburbanite demands.

*Destroyed in 1955.
†William Willet was a late Victorian builder. He developed the south side of Sloane Street and was a leading advocate of daylight saving.

Tower Bridge and Planners

SPECTATOR. 20 DECEMBER 1957

An MP said in Parliament last week that the Tower Bridge would have to be taken down in twenty or thirty years and that he personally would like to see it demolished tomorrow. I wonder how far we are right, whatever our aesthetic opinions, in taking down something that is a landmark to millions of people and part of their lives. The Tower Bridge to millions means London and the Pool of London. It was designed by dear old Sir Horace Jones in 1886–94, and he was so fat that a crescent had to be carved out of the council table of the RIBA when he was president of that institution. Sir Horace had long dreamed of a bascule bridge at this point and in Sir John Wolfe Barry he found the engineer to realise his vision. The Tower Bridge may dwarf the Tower of London, its pinnacled Gothic (recently, alas, shorn of the ironwork weather vanes and miniature flèches which gave an elegant finish to the design) may be coarse and incorrect, but the Tower Bridge has guts and outline and real grandeur. At dawn or sunset it is unforgettable, the real gateway to the greatest city in the world. I cannot believe that a new bridge further down or up stream cannot relieve some of the traffic. Who is this pseudo-progressive MP who wants to interfere with London? I wish I could remember his name. When Sir Horace was designing the bridge his chief draughtsman, the father of Sir Frank Brangwyn, had spent most of his life in Belgium, which may account for the Flemish look of its towers.

I think the reason why people dislike the word 'planning' and those connected with it is not because they object to new towns or to flowering cherries and civic centres, but because in their minds planning is associated with destruction. Bombing we can take. Fire may be carelessness. But the deliberate pulling down of a familiar street or building with associations, the felling of timber in a village and the destruction of old cottages is really playing about with part of ourselves. They are roots and home to somebody. I have always noticed that progressive architects and planners and, no doubt, the chief shareholders in those sinister development trusts which are buying up London and ruining it with oblong up-ended packing cases live in old houses and go to a good deal of trouble to protect their views. If someone starts to destroy the Tower Bridge, real Londoners, and there are many left, will rise against their suburban dictators.

HIGHGATE AND OUT TO THE SUBURBS

In Highgate Cemetery

Millfield Lane

Summoned By Bells

Here on the southern slope of Highgate Hill
Red squirrels leap the hornbeams. Still I see
Twigs and serrated leaves against the sky.
The sunny silence was of Middlesex.
Once a Delauney-Belleville crawling up
West Hill in bottom gear made such a noise
As drew me from my dream-world out to watch
That early motor-car attempt the steep.
But mostly it was footsteps, rustling leaves,
And blackbirds fluting over miles of Heath.
    Then Millfield Lane looked like a Constable
And all the grassy hillocks spoke of Keats.
Mysterious gravel drives to hidden wealth
Wound between laurels – mighty Caenwood Towers
And Grand Duke Michael's house and Holly Lodge.

Highgate and Hampstead

Preface to Leonard Clarke: PROSPECT OF
HIGHGATE AND HAMPSTEAD. 1967

It astonishes me how little Highgate and Hampstead have changed com-
pared with other suburbs in the last fifty years. Certain things of my childhood there have disappeared; the Burdett Coutts estate on West Hill and
the red squirrels; the flocks of sheep which used to come up from the
Heath; the road-sweepers who collected a sack of horse chestnuts for me
in the autumn; buttercups and dandelions which used to grow in the
Heath grass before it was sprayed with weed killer; the old woman who
sold humbugs by the railway bridge at Gospel Oak. Then of course the
sounds have changed. Instead of the muffin man with his bell, the coal
cart, the stable clocks, rumble of iron rims over grit, horses' hooves, the
distant hoots and puffs of the North London steam trains, there is now the
universal roar of the internal combustion engine on the earth, and of jets
in the sky.

The scenery remains much the same. Though they have been called 'in
London' the twin villages are still Middlesex country, and a memory of
that distinguished little county with its dark brownish-red brick cedar-
shaded garden walls, eighteenth-century iron gates leading to merchants'
houses who had set themselves up as squires in Georgian times. Near the
brick houses still survive weather-boarded cottages, and Hampstead even
more than Highgate is rich in those cheerful stucco houses of late
Georgian and early Victorian date.

Both villages have been spared the rush of mid-war development which
destroyed most of the rest of Middlesex. It was largely because with
remarkable foresight in the last century the Metropolitan Board of Works
purchased the Heath from a private landlord.

From that Heath it is still possible to see the views which Constable
painted, of elms, ponds and sandy hollows, and the far blue hills of
Surrey to the South, though the dome of Paul's between them and here is
now hidden by developers' slabs. It is still possible on an autumn evening
in Flask Walk, or Well Walk, or Millfield Lane, or Fitzroy Park, to get the
atmosphere which inspired Keats and made Middlesex into Greece for
him. The village quality comes back most on a snowy public holiday when
traffic is deadened.

South Kentish Town

Broadcast on the Home Service of the BBC, in January 1951.

This is a story about a very unimportant station on the Underground railway in London. It was devastatingly unimportant. I remember it quite well. It was called 'South Kentish Town'* and its entrance was on the Kentish Town Road, a busy street full of shops. Omnibuses and tramcars passed the entrance every minute, but they never stopped. True, there was a notice saying 'STOP HERE IF REQUIRED' outside the station. But no one required, so nothing stopped.

Hardly anyone used the station at all. I should think about three people a day. Every other train on the Underground railway went through without stopping: 'Passing South Kentish Town!' Passengers used Camden Town Station to the south of it, and Kentish Town to the north of it, but South Kentish Town they regarded as an unnecessary interpolation, like a comma in the wrong place in a sentence, or an uncalled-for remark in the middle of an interesting story. When trains stopped at South Kentish Town the passengers were annoyed.

Poor South Kentish Town. But we need not be very sorry for it. It had its uses. It was a rest-home for tired ticket-collectors who were also liftmen: in those days there were no moving stairways as they had not been invented. 'George,' the Station Master at Leicester Square would say, 'You've been collecting a thousand tickets an hour here for the last six months. You can go and have a rest at South Kentish Town.' And gratefully George went.

Then progress came along, as, alas, it so often does: and progress, as you know, means doing away with anything restful and useless. There was an amalgamation of the Underground railways and progressive officials decided that South Kentish Town should be shut. So the lifts were wheeled out of their gates and taken away by road in lorries. The great black shafts were boarded over at the top; as was the winding spiral staircase up from the Underground station. This staircase had been built in case the lifts went wrong – all old Underground stations have them. The whole entrance part of the station was turned into shops. All you noticed as you rolled by in a tramcar down the Kentish Town Road was something that looked like an Underground station, but when you looked again it was two shops, a tobacconist's and a coal-merchant's. Down below they

*South Kentish Town Station opened on the Northern Line in 1907. It closed on 5 June 1924 as the result of a strike at Lots Road Power Station and never re-opened.

switched off the lights on the platforms and in the passages leading to the lifts, and then they left the station to itself. The only way you could know, if you were in an Underground train, that there had ever been a South Kentish Town Station, was that the train made a different noise as it rushed through the dark and empty platform. It went quieter with a sort of swoosh instead of a roar and if you looked out of the window you could see the lights of the carriages reflected in the white tiles of the station wall.

Well now comes the terrible story I have to tell. You must imagine for a moment Mr Basil Green. He was an income tax official who lived in N.6 which was what he called that part of London where he and Mrs Green had a house. He worked in Whitehall from where he sent out letters asking for money (with threat of imprisonment if it was not paid). Some of this money he kept himself, but most of it he gave to politicians to spend on progress. Of course it was quite all right, Mr Green writing these threatening letters as people felt they ought to have them. That is democracy. Every weekday morning of his life Mr Green travelled from Kentish Town to the Strand reading the *News Chronicle*. Every weekday evening of his life he travelled back from the Strand to Kentish Town reading the *Evening Standard*. He always caught exactly the same train. He always wore exactly the same sort of black clothes and carried an umbrella. He did not smoke and only drank lime-juice or cocoa. He always sent out exactly the same letters to strangers, demanding money with threats. He had been very pleased when they shut South Kentish Town Station because it shortened his journey home by one stop. And the nice thing about Mr Basil Green was that he loved Mrs Green his wife and was always pleased to come back to her in their little house, where she had a nice hot meal ready for him.

Mr Basil Green was such a methodical man, always doing the same thing every day, that he did not have to look up from his newspaper on the Underground journey. A sort of clock inside his head told him when he had reached the Strand in the morning. The same clock told him he had reached Kentish Town in the evening.

Then one Friday night two extraordinary things happened. First there was a hitch on the line so that the train stopped in the tunnel exactly beside the deserted and empty platform of South Kentish Town Station. Second, the man who worked the automatic doors of the Underground carriages pushed a button and opened them. I suppose he wanted to see what was wrong. Anyhow, Mr Green, his eyes intent on the *Evening Standard*, got up from his seat. The clock in his head said 'First stop after Camden Town, Kentish Town.' Still reading the *Evening Standard* he got up and stepped out of the open door on to what he thought was going to be Kentish Town platform, without looking about him. And before anyone could call Mr Green back, the man at the other end of the train who worked the automatic doors, shut them and the train moved on. Mr Green found himself standing on a totally dark platform, ALONE.

'My hat!' said Mr Green, 'wrong station. No lights? Where am I? This must be *South* Kentish Town. Lordy! I must stop the next train. I'll be at least three minutes late!'

So there in the darkness he waited. Presently he heard the rumble of an oncoming train, so he put his newspaper into his pocket, straightened himself up and waved his umbrella up and down in front of the train.

The train whooshed past without taking any notice and disappeared into the tunnel towards Kentish Town with a diminishing roar. 'I know,' thought Mr Green, 'my umbrella's black so the driver could not see it. Next time I'll wave my *Evening Standard*. It's white and he'll see that.'

The next train came along. He waved the newspaper, but nothing happened. What was he to do? Six minutes late now. Mrs Green would be getting worried. So he decided to cross through the dark tunnel to the other platform. 'They may be less in a hurry over there', he thought. But he tried to stop two trains and still no one would take any notice of him. 'Quite half an hour late now! Oh dear, this is awful. I know – there must be a staircase out of this empty station. I wish I had a torch. I wish I smoked and had a box of matches. As it is I will have to feel my way.' So carefully he walked along until the light of a passing train showed him an opening off the platform.

In utter darkness he mounted some stairs and, feeling along the shiny tiled walls of the passage at the top of the short flight, came to the spiral staircase of the old emergency exit of South Kentish Town Station. Up and up and up he climbed; up and up and round and round for 294 steps. Then he hit his head a terrific whack. He had bumped it against the floor of one of the shops, and through the boards he could hear the roar of traffic on the Kentish Town Road. Oh how he wished he were out of all this darkness and up in the friendly noisy street. But there seemed to be nobody in the shop above, which was natural as it was the coal-merchant's and there wasn't any coal. He banged at the floorboards with his umbrella with all his might, but he banged in vain, so there was nothing for it but to climb all the way down those 294 steps again. And when he reached the bottom Mr Green heard the trains roaring through the dark station and he felt hopeless.

He decided next to explore the lift shafts. Soon he found them, and there at the top, as though from the bottom of a deep, deep well, was a tiny chink of light. It was shining through the floorboards of the tobacconist's shop. But how was he to reach it?

I don't know whether you know what the lift shafts of London's Underground railways are like. They are enormous – twice as big as this room where I am sitting and round instead of square. All the way round them are iron ledges jutting out about six inches from the iron walls and each ledge is about two feet above the next. A brave man could swing himself on to one of these and climb up hand over hand, if he were sensible enough not to look down and make himself giddy.

By now Mr Basil Green was desperate. He *must* get home to dear Mrs Green. That ray of light in the floorboards away up at the top of the shaft was his chance of attracting attention and getting home. So deliberately and calmly he laid down his evening paper and his umbrella at the entrance to the shaft and swung himself on to the bottom ledge. And slowly he began to climb. As he went higher and higher, the rumble of the trains passing through the station hundreds of feet below grew fainter. He thought he heard once again the friendly noise of traffic up in the Kentish Town Road. Yes, he *did* hear it, for the shop door was, presumably, open. He heard it distinctly and there was the light clear enough. He was nearly there, nearly at the top, but not quite. For just as he was about to knock the floorboard with his knuckles while he held desperately on to the iron ledge with his other hand there was a click and the light went out. Feet above his head trod away from him and a door banged. The noise of the traffic was deadened, and far, far away below him he caught the rumble, now loud and now disappearing, of the distant, heedless trains.

I will not pain you with a description of how Mr Green climbed very slowly down the lift shaft again. You will know how much harder it is to climb down anything than it is to climb up it. All I will tell you is that when he eventually arrived at the bottom, two hours later, he was wet with sweat and he had been sweating as much with fright as with exertion.

And when he did get to the bottom, Mr Green felt for his umbrella and his *Evening Standard* and crawled slowly to the station where he lay down on the dark empty platform. The trains rushed through to Kentish Town as he made a pillow for his head from the newspaper and placed his umbrella by his side. He cried a little with relief that he was at any rate still alive, but mostly with sorrow for thinking of how terribly worried Mrs Green would be. The meal would be cold. She would be thinking he was killed and ringing up the police. 'Oh Violette!' he sobbed, 'Violette!' He pronounced her name Veeohlet because it was a French name though Mrs Green was English. 'Oh Violette! Shall I ever see you again?'

It was now about half past ten at night and the trains were getting fewer and fewer and the empty station seemed emptier and darker so that he almost welcomed the oncoming rumble of those cruel trains which still rushed past. They were at any rate kinder than the dreadful silence in the station when they had gone away and he could imagine huge hairy spiders or reptiles in the dark passages by which he had so vainly tried to make his escape . . .

Parliament Hill Fields

Rumbling under blackened girders, Midland, bound for Cricklewood,
Puffed its sulphur to the sunset where that Lane of Laundries stood.
Rumble under, thunder over, train and tram alternate go,
Shake the floor and smudge the ledger, Charrington, Sells, Dale and Co.,
Nuts and nuggets in the window, trucks along the lines below.

When the Bon Marché was shuttered, when the feet were hot and tired,
Outside Charrington's we waited, by the "STOP HERE IF REQUIRED",
Launched aboard the shopping basket, sat precipitately down,
Rocked past Zwanziger the baker's, and the terrace blackish brown,
And the curious Anglo-Norman parish church of Kentish Town.

Till the tram went over thirty, sighting terminus again,
Past municipal lawn tennis and the bobble-hanging plane;
Soft the light suburban evening caught our ashlar-speckled spire,
Eighteen-sixty Early English, as the mighty elms retire
Either side of Brookfield Mansions flashing fine French-window fire.

Oh the after-tram-ride quiet, when we heard a mile beyond,
Silver music from the bandstand, barking dogs by Highgate Pond;
Up the hill where stucco houses in Virginia creeper drown—
And my childish wave of pity, seeing children carrying down
Sheaves of drooping dandelions to the courts of Kentish Town.

In 1971, in reply to a member of the Camden History Society asking about details in the poem above, Betjeman wrote:

The tram is a number 7 and it was brown when it was L.C.C. I can just remember the horse trams which were open on top and always longed to clutch one of those bobbles that hung temptingly near from the plane trees.

Hampstead Heath then had buttercups and daisies and dandelions in the grass at the Parliament Hill Fields end. Daniels was a kind of Selfridges and it was on the corner of Prince of Wales's Road, or very near that corner. There was a cinema higher up on the same side and there I saw my first films, very early animated pictures, it was called the "Electric

Palace". Then a grander cinema was built between Daniels and the Prince of Wales's Road. My father who was deaf very much liked going to silent films here and he took me with him. The Bon Marché was an old fashioned drapers' shop with about three fronts north of the cinema and opposite Kentish Town Underground Station was a Penny Bazaar and next to that was Zwanziger which always smelt of baking bread. Here too was the tram stop for the last stage of the route north. Then there was an antique dealer and picture framer called Yewlett and a public house. My father visited the former but not the latter.

Then there was some late Georgian brick houses with steps up to their front doors, then the always-locked parish church of Kentish Town. (That was the one I referred to in the poem. It was rebuilt in Norman style in 1843 by J. H. Hakewill and seems to have no dedication.) It was very low. Then there was Maples' warehouse, always rather grim, then some squalid shops and a grocer's shop called Wailes which was very old-fashioned. Then came Highgate Road Station with a smell of steam and very rare trains which ran, I think, to Southend from a terminus at Gospel Oak. Then there were some rather grander shops with a definite feeling of suburbia; Young the Chemist on the corner (Young had a collie dog); Pedder the oil and colourman; and French for provisions; then Gordon House, grim behind its high gray walls. I remember thinking how beautiful the new bits of Metroland Villas were in the newly built Glenhurst Avenue, and my father telling me they were awful. Then there were the red brick gloom of Lissenden Gardens and Parliament Hill Mansions. I was born at 52 but moved to West Hill as a baby so cannot recall the flats. Where the school is now there were trees, but they were not part of Parliament Hill Fields.

I could go on like this for ever, but I must stop or I shall arrive at 31 West Hill. It was very countrified. My greatest thrill was to walk with my father down a place in Kentish Town called Faulkner's Lane. I then thought it was a slum, but now realise it was charming Middlesex Cottages. It was a little village south of the Great Eastern and on the east side of Kentish Town Road. I remember going with my mother to visit a 'poor family' in Anglers' Lane, Kentish Town. The only toys the children had to play with were pieces of wood from a bundle of kindling.

Highgate Hill

Three verses from

'An Incident in the Early Life of Ebenezer Jones, Poet, 1828'

The lumber of a London-going dray,
The still-new stucco on the London clay,
Hot summer silence over Holloway.

Dissenting chapels, tea-bowers, lovers' lairs,
Neat new-built villas, ample Grecian squares,
Remaining orchards ripening Windsor pears.

Hot silence where the older mansions hide
On Highgate Hill's thick elm-encrusted side,
And Pancras, Hornsey, Islington divide.

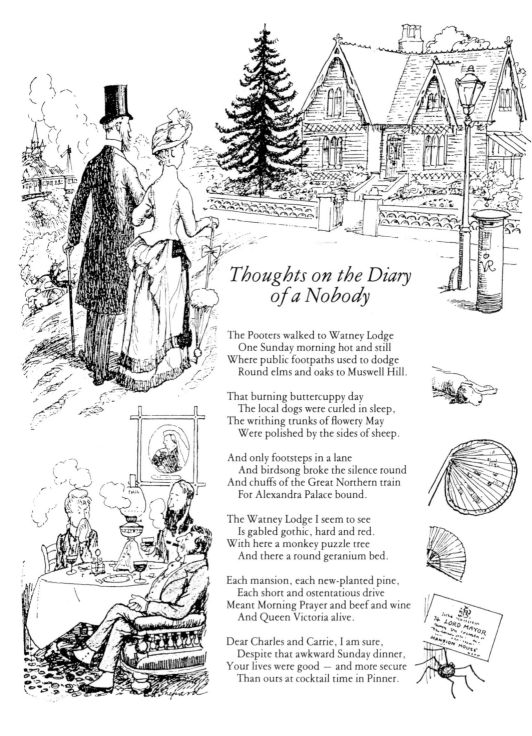

Thoughts on the Diary of a Nobody

The Pooters walked to Watney Lodge
  One Sunday morning hot and still
Where public footpaths used to dodge
  Round elms and oaks to Muswell Hill.

That burning buttercuppy day
  The local dogs were curled in sleep,
The writhing trunks of flowery May
  Were polished by the sides of sheep.

And only footsteps in a lane
  And birdsong broke the silence round
And chuffs of the Great Northern train
  For Alexandra Palace bound.

The Watney Lodge I seem to see
  Is gabled gothic, hard and red.
With here a monkey puzzle tree
  And there a round geranium bed.

Each mansion, each new-planted pine,
  Each short and ostentatious drive
Meant Morning Prayer and beef and wine
  And Queen Victoria alive.

Dear Charles and Carrie, I am sure,
  Despite that awkward Sunday dinner,
Your lives were good — and more secure
  Than ours at cocktail time in Pinner.

The Most Significant Suburb – Bedford Park

DAILY TELEGRAPH. 22 AUGUST 1960

The word suburb means an outlying district to a town. But no one in London in, say, 1684, when Barbon laid out Red Lion Square, or when 18th-century squares such as Grosvenor, Cavendish and Smith were added to the Metropolis – not even some one living in the Old Town at Edinburgh when the New Town was rising clean and spacious on a nearby hill – would have thought of calling the dwellers in these places sub-urbanites. The 18th-century idea of a suburb was an extension of the town into the fields. What we have come to think of as suburbs, alas in a faintly derogatory sense, is the opposite idea, a late 18th-century romantic idea. Instead of straight lines there were curves, instead of sym-metry, irregularity. The dweller in the romantic suburb was to live in a detached house in a garden of his own. Neighbouring gardens were to give the illusion of being an extension of his own garden. Each man was his own squire with his own short carriage drive and park.

This exactly suited the merchant of the industrial towns of the North and the big cities of the South. Every town dweller in Britain in the last century was little more than one generation removed from some country village where his family originated. Instead of a cottage he could now afford a villa and if he was not entitled to a coat of arms on his carriage and over his front door he could at least have stained glass on the hall stairs and spikes and turrets on his roof.

The railway could take him to his work and he could be at home with his wife and children in the evenings in what seemed like country. The suburb was the fulfilment of every man's dream – a house of his own in the country.

A precedent for it had been set in Georgian times by such schemes as the layout of detached houses on the Eyre estate in St John's Wood, London, started in 1794, and John Nash's Park Villages circa 1830. But the houses here were too small for the suddenly enriched Victorian indus-trialists; consequently we have residential districts like Streatham and Lewisham in London, the Park in Nottingham, Jesmond Dene in Newcastle-on-Tyne, Mossley Hill in Liverpool, Edgbaston in Birming-ham, Roundhay in Leeds, Morningside in Edinburgh, Kelvinside in Glasgow and Whalley Range in Manchester.

Gas lamps and possibly a lodge at the entrance, laurels along the drive (in which Sherlock Holmes might be hiding with his bull's-eye lantern),

Bath Road, Bedford Park

red paper in the dining room and heavy mahogany chairs, green paper in the billiard room, pale silk on the drawing room walls and armour in the hall – what are they now, these merchants' dreams of home? Clinics, branches of the public library, Ministry of Pensions offices, and their gardens filled with huts or new villas built in a feeble attempt to look like Frank Lloyd Wright. And where are they now, the sons and grandsons of these merchant princes? Expenses farmers in the Home Counties or fishers in the Scottish lochs.

I think these mid-Victorian suburbs were jeered at because they were symbols of class distinction. The old land-owning classes despised them because they were not real country, the sweated-workers of the industrial towns envied them.

They themselves were built when the middle classes were riddled with subtle distinctions. The wholesaler looked down on the retailer, the attorney and the doctor looked down on the merchant whether wholesale or retail because he was in trade. Only clergymen and peers were above criticism; even bankers were suspect.

The most significant suburb built in the last century, probably the most significant in the Western world, is Bedford Park, Chiswick, laid out in 1876 by Norman Shaw. It was designed specially for 'artistic people of moderate incomes'. It stands in orchard land and the picturesque brick houses with their faintly Dutch look are late Victorian versions of the small parsonage houses which were built in the heyday of the Gothic revival a generation earlier.

Bedford Park was built to be self-contained: it has a church, and what was once a co-operative store. The Tabard Inn with William de Morgan tiles in the public bar and a hall panelled with cedar from a demolished city church, was where men could play the clavichord to ladies in tussore dresses, and where supporters of William Morris could learn of early Socialism.

Here Yeats as a young man lived with his artist father. Here until just before the war gentle crafts-folk survived making Celtic jewellery in their studios or weaving on hand looms among the faded sun flowers of a now forgotten cult.

It is sad that the winding roads of this leafy garden suburb are now cut through by heavy traffic and that the fences so carefully designed as part of the whole composition are dilapidated or altered. But the spirit of Bedford Park is still there and it is probably one of our most charming and important monuments; nor is its usefulness past. Many of its roads are very pleasant to live in.

Bedford Park was the origin of many another garden suburb. Enlightened manufacturers, spurred on by the ideals of early Socialism and with that social conscience which Non-conformity and Christian Socialism in the Church of England gave to the late Victorians, built garden suburbs for their workers.

In 1892, Ebenezer Howard started the idea of garden cities which were an extension of the Bedford Park experiment, and Letchworth was begun in 1903. Hampstead Garden Suburb was started in 1907 with its charming houses by Barry Parker and Raymond Unwin and the Lutyens churches. In these places the houses were more cottage-like than those of Bedford Park, the old village rather than its parsonage was the model. Welwyn, begun in 1919, was an even bolder experiment with its own industries and houses in a Georgian style.

A suburb, provided it is not too consciously community centred, can be a pleasant place to live in – quiet, clean and full of vistas. Above everything it is human and respects the individual. This cannot be said of the tall blocks of workers' flats going up today which are conceived in terms of density, plot ratio and cost to the rates.

Narcissus

(the first verse)

Yes, it was Bedford Park the vision came from —
   de Morgan lustre glowing round the hearth,
And that sweet flower which self-love takes its name from
   Nodding among the lilies in the garth,
And Arnold Dolmetsch touching the spinet,
And Mother, Chiswick's earliest suffragette.

Arnold Dolmetsch and his family

THE CITY

All silvery on frosty nights
Were City steeples white against the stars.
And narrowly the chasms wound between
Italianate counting-houses, Roman banks,
To this church and that. Huge office-doors
Their granite thresholds worn by weekday feet
(Now far away in slippered ease at Penge),
Stood locked. St. Botolph this, St. Mary that
Alone shone out resplendent in the dark.
SUMMONED BY BELLS

*John Betjeman looking at Cloth Fair from
the churchyard of St Bartholomew's*

John Betjeman's study at Cloth Fair

Living in the City

THE OBSERVER COLOUR SUPPLEMENT. 24 JULY 1977

This was the nicest place in London to live in because everything could be reached on foot, down alleys and passages. Like all county towns it had a bit of every trade. I was lucky enough to live in Cloth Fair where there was still a shop which sold cloth. On some weekly nights there was bell-ringing from the Tower of St Bartholomew's the Great, just such bells as the walled city must have heard when there were 108 churches in its square mile. Behind me was Smithfield meat market* with its cheerful Chaucerian characters and medieval-looking hand barrows. The hellish noise of articulated lorries coming in from Europe in the small hours drove me out. Just over the boundary were the rag trade and the print and down in Clerkenwell the clocks. Southward, the City became a river port with wharves and cobbled quays and a smell of fish from Billingsgate where alleys plunged steeply to the river.

There was still a sense of sewers where Fleet Ditch flows under Farringdon Street and Fleet Street climbs westward through the journalists to the Temple and the Law. East of the City at Aldgate Pump I could sense the Orient, and at Beaver Hall on a Sunday business was brisk in the fur trade while the rest of London was silent. What makes the City so different from all London is its secrecy. It is really a village of about 400 people who know each other and whose words are their bond. If they break their word they are out. All this secret life is sealed by those medieval guilds, the City companies with their livery halls, bumbledom and beadles.

The character of the City has been nearly killed by old-fashioned tower blocks and inhuman scale.

*Two schemes for developing Smithfield market are currently under consideration by Tower Hamlets Council.

[43]

St. Bartholomew's Hospital

The ghost of Rahere still walks in Bart's;
It gives an impulse to generous hearts,
It looks on pain with a pitying eye,
It teaches us never to fear to die.

Eight hundred years of compassion and care
Have hallowed its fountain, stones and Square.
Pray for us all as we near the gate —
St. Bart the Less and St. Bart the Great.

The City Churches

SPECTATOR. 5 NOVEMBER 1954

In the London Museum, when it was at Lancaster House, there used to be a delightful dark tunnel of models of old London, including one of the Great Fire itself. These models have lost their intimacy and character in the arid apple-green quarters of the new London Museum which is in the duller rooms of Kensington Palace.* But it is still possible, by kneeling at the models so that the houses are at eye level, to imagine oneself back in the medieval City, where every house seemed to look like a cross between Staple Inn and Lavenham and where there were 108 City churches.

With this picture of a walled city, with red roofs and white stone and many turrets and a wide, slow-flowing Thames, held up from the sea by the sluice of waters under London Bridge, leave Kensington and go to Aldersgate Street. By going under the arch of the Star Inn in that street and turning left among the parked motors, you can still come out into the country. Silence reigns and bracken and willow-herb and a few saplings grow among grass which covers a multitude of basements. A footpath toward the Middlesex-looking tower of St Giles's, Cripplegate, leads in this country quiet to some large remains of the City wall.[†] And as you see this great wall stretching ruinously towards Moorgate you can imagine yourself once more in the fields outside the ancient City. Though there are eight City churches which have survived, or at any rate partly survived, both the Great Fire and the German bombs, only two of them, I think, bring back medieval London – St Bartholomew the Great and St Ethelburga, Bishopsgate. The venerable and blackened Norman interior of St Bartholomew's is not improved by cement vaulting in the aisles and by the plethora of chairs, postcard tables, vases, brooms, ladders and other semi-sacred impedimenta of our dear old Church of England, and I really catch more of an idea of what the old churches of London before the Fire may have looked like from the humble little church of St Ethelburga.

Wren rebuilt fifty churches after the fire. Before the Germans came we had ourselves destroyed nineteen of these. The Germans completely gutted seventeen more Wren churches and there are now only fourteen with their roofs on, and of these three are still shut to the public, which

---

*The London Museum moved to its present site, 150, London Wall, EC2, in 1977.

[†] As John Betjeman later wrote, St Giles Cripplegate is now 'the only church among the glassy slabs of the Barbican scheme.'

leaves us with eleven Wren churches open to us in the City, and precious indeed they are. Under the Archdeacon of London's farsighted plan for the City churches, many more will be opened later when they are repaired or rebuilt.

Of those which survive for seeing today, I commend St Benet, Paul's Wharf, which is Welsh and inclined to be locked, St Mary-at-Hill, St Magnus the Martyr, St Margaret, Lothbury, St Margaret Pattens, St Peter, Cornhill, and St Stephen's, Walbrook, as being the most characteristic Wren churches, comparatively unmolested by Victorian 'restoration'. St Mary-at-Hill, which is nothing to look at outside and surrounded by a smell of fish at Billingsgate,* has the most untouched interior of all. Here the box pews, ironwork sword-rests, great west gallery, with its rich organ case, the fine pulpit and sounding board, the carved altar and altar-piece, recall Georgian London when beadles would hit the charity children sitting in the gallery with their staves, when merchants lived over their shops and offices and pageboys carried the prayer books of rich widows before them as they walked to worship.

There were more such unrestored churches in the City nearly forty years ago when I first knew it, for as a young boy I delighted to visit City churches, especially on a Sunday evening when single bells beat from moonlit steeples down gas-lit alleys, and choirboys would rush round corners through vestry archways. I can remember the row of fish-tail gas lights all along the triforium of St Bartholomew the Great; St Magnus the Martyr, when it had box pews and seemed very dead, unlike the live and coloured place it is today; and St Alban, Wood Street, with its green gas mantles and sparse congregation. In those days too, aged City men would come down from their brick, Italianate houses in Highbury or Streatham to worship in the City church where their fathers had worshipped before them. It was always my hope on some dark night to find a church which had escaped all the guide books and was there still in its classic splendour, with candles reflected in polished oak and cedar, with a parson in a black gown and bands, a beadle and the court of a City Company, robed and carrying a mace and swords. Once I thought I really had found the destroyed Wren church of St Matthew, Friday Street. Where is the oratory of Prebendary Hine-Haycock, preaching to the ranks of Blue Coat boys, tier upon tier in the galleries of Christ Church, Newgate Street? Where is the dome of St Mildred, Bread Street, under which I sat in a high pew to hear the words of the Reverend Mr Richardson-Eyre, who would come in from some comfortable suburb to preach at Evensong on Sunday evening? Where is St Stephen, Coleman Street, the plainest and most despised of Wren's churches? Where the Evangelical raptures I enjoyed in St

*Billingsgate fish market closed in 1982. The buildings have been converted into a shopping centre.

[47]

Bride's? Gone, gone, dead and bombed, only their peaceful memory now part of the history of our beautiful City. Yet the bombing has done one service to Wren which makes up for the destruction which tall buildings and the commercial policy of the Church have done to his forest of steeples gathered round St Paul's. If you stand at the corner of Wood Street near the back of Goldsmiths Hall, in the morning light or at night when the moon is up and there is a faint red glow in the sky from the West End, you will see what must be one of the most beautiful architectural sights in England. In the foreground withered willow-herb almost buries a pile of huge pink stones. Beyond this is Wren's exquisite stone steeple of St Vedast, Foster Lane, less elaborate but more satisfying than his famous steeple of St Mary-le-Bow, which stands quite near. Beyond St Vedast you will see the mighty dome of St Paul's and to the right the delicate and complicated silhouette of the north-west bell tower. And as you walk down Wood Street to Cheapside, St Vedast's steeple will glide past them

and the hollows in it will open to show the sky beyond. Here architecture does what all the best architecture should do. It moves as you go past it and changes to make another and another and another perfect picture.

I have left to the last those City churches built since the time of Wren and which architecturally are some of the best and, though I dare to say it, more impressive and inventive as interiors than those by Wren himself. I think the first indignation at vandalism I ever felt was over the destruction of the eighteenth-century brick church of St Catherine Coleman, Fenchurch Street, which happened between the wars. In those days people could swallow Wren but nothing later. Georgian was thought little of and St Catherine's was a complete untouched Georgian interior, with all its old woodwork. Since then, thank goodness, our appreciation has widened. But the Church has destroyed eight of the seventeen post-Wren churches in the City of London. Mercifully the Germans did little damage to three of the best, St Mary Woolnoth, All Hallows, London Wall, and St Botolph, Aldersgate. Hawksmoor's church of St Mary

Woolnoth by the Bank, with its twin square towers, is surely one of the most brilliant solutions to an awkwardly shaped site one could hope to see. The windowless side walls are full of interest. The interior, with its top lights, though it is in fact small, seems majestic and enormous. What is it that makes the City so different from all the rest of London? Mostly I think the City is different because of its churches, and these are used today more than ever, not just for concerts but as places in which to pray. If you go into the newly opened church of St James's, Piccadilly, you will find plenty of people about, but they are most of them standing and admiring the ornament. If you go into a City church you will generally find someone on his knees.

'City Forenoon' by Osbert Lancaster

[49]

A *Salvo for Cannon Street*

SPECTATOR. 2 DECEMBER 1955

Cannon Street Station,* which was designed by Edward Myddleton Barry in the early Sixties, may yet be saved. Its terminal towers on the river, with their lead steeples, are a great adornment to the City skyline, and seem to me to equal in elegance and ingenuity the lead domes and spirelets of Wren's City churches, to which they form so admirable a foreground from the river and Southwark. That vast, echoing interior, whose great cast-iron roof has been allowed to remain unglazed and uncared-for since that fatal Act of Parliament brought British Railways into being, will presumably come down first. You, who have the honour of getting out at Cannon Street, look and see how cleverly Barry has made the curve of the roof fit into the design of the façade of the hotel on this, the station side. It will brighten your Monday morning for you and make you proud to realise that the railways of England produced some of the best architecture of the past century, and were not furtive, gimcrack and cheeseparing as they have become today under the British Transport Commission.

*The roof, which was damaged in the War, was removed, leaving the curtain walls and towers on the river looking rather bereft, when the station booking hall was redesigned in the 1960s. A new proposal to build between the curtain walls, glazing in the blank arches, has recently been proposed.

Monody on the Death of Aldersgate Street Station

Snow falls in the buffet of Aldersgate station,
  Soot hangs in the tunnel in clouds of steam.
City of London! before the next desecration
  Let your steepled forest of churches be my theme.

Sunday Silence! with every street a dead street,
  Alley and courtyard empty and cobbled mews,
Till "tingle tang" the bell of St. Mildred's Bread Street
  Summoned the sermon taster to high box pews,

And neighbouring towers and spirelets joined the ringing
  With answering echoes from heavy commercial walls
Till all were drowned as the sailing clouds went singing
  On the roaring flood of a twelve-voiced peal from Paul's.

Then would the years fall off and Thames run slowly,
  Out into marshy meadow land flowed the Fleet,
And the walled-in City of London, smelly and holy,
  Had a tinkling mass house in every cavernous street.

The bells rang down and St. Michael Paternoster
  Would take me into its darkness from College Hill,
Or Christ Church Newgate Street (with St. Leonard Foster)
  Would be late for Mattins and ringing insistent still.

Last of the east wall sculpture, a cherub gazes
  On broken arches, rosebay, bracken and dock,
Where once I heard the roll of the Prayer Book phrases
  And the sumptuous tick of the old west gallery clock.

Snow falls in the buffet of Aldersgate station,
  Toiling and doomed from Moorgate Street puffs the train,
For us of the steam and the gas-light, the lost generation,
  The new white cliffs of the City are built in vain.*

*The arches and span of the original building were
  destroyed when it became the Barbican station.

[51]

John Betjeman in the Coal Exchange

Round the Exchanges

SPECTATOR. 13 APRIL 1956

I did a tour this week of the Exchanges of the City of London. The most crowded is the Stock Exchange. From the public gallery, which is a glass tank almost in the ceiling of the building, one looks down on a nest of black ants and a few dark blue ones and a very few wearing bowler hats, all walking among litter like Newlands Corner after a Bank Holiday. Their movements seemed purposeless, and when one of them shouts none of the others takes any notice. The weirdest Exchange is the Wool Exchange,* whose entrance in Basinghall Street, designed about 1860, is modern architecture before its time. Inside it is a labyrinth of cast-iron staircases, passages and sky-lights. In fifteen years, when its lease is up, I suppose we shall have to do battle to save this dream-like building, a real relic of Mr Pooter's London. The most beautiful Exchange is the Coal Exchange opposite Billingsgate, designed by J. B. Bunning (1846–9). Its great domed interior is one of the very best in the City, impressive, vast and exquisitely detailed. The stanchions of cast-iron supporting the galleries are made of a cable motif, the paintings on the panels, by Sang, show Victorian industrial scenes (some of them have been wantonly 'creamed over'). I am told this building is threatened, for the dead hand of the Coal Board is over it and no longer do coal merchants transact their business on its tessellated floor.† The Royal Exchange has become a museum. It was opened by Queen Elizabeth, and Tite's sumptuous structure is the third building on the site. But that great courtyard has to be kept open in perpetuity and the constables who open and shut it and stand there all day are employed by the Gresham Committee, which, with the Mercers' Company, looks after the building. If you've been hammered out of the Stock Exchange, hauled out of the Coal Exchange and sacked from the Wool Exchange you can still do business in the Royal Exchange.

*Demolished in 1963 and later replaced by an office block called Woolgate House.
† The Coal Exchange was destroyed in 1962.

St Paul's

DAILY TELEGRAPH. 23 MAY 1957

On certain Tuesday evenings in the month, when all the office workers have gone home and before the meat and fish markets have started their midnight thunder, the 12 bells of St Paul's are most beautifully rung for practice. Their notes, deep as an organ, pour over the empty offices and the towers and steeples of lesser churches and remind one that the City is the real old London, with its medieval lanes and courts, its ancient Guilds and little parishes.

The sound of the bells brings back Old St Paul's before it was destroyed in the fire of 1666. It was the longest cathedral in England and in all Europe only St Peter's, Milan and Seville surpassed it in size. The golden eagle over its central spire dominated the flat Thames valley for miles, and the huge Gothic church rose high over the close-packed, clustering houses. The Cathedral was the social centre of the city. Here, in the early morning, Mass was said daily at more than 30 lighted altars for the souls of the departed, while at the high altar the Mass of the people was celebrated. Behind high screens in the choir the Offices of the Church were said throughout the day. The great nave of the church, the people's part, was full of hubbub so that the priests in the choir could hardly hear themselves say their offices. The nave was law courts, exchange, hiring-place and general meeting place of the City, infested with beggars and thieves as well as the respectable. Outside, at a stone octagon called Paul's Cross, sermons were preached on current abuses. Here Latimer inveighed against mercantile morals, here popery was denounced.

After reading a new history of St Paul's, edited by Dr W. R. Matthews, Dean of St Paul's, and the Rev. W. M. Atkins, the Cathedral's Librarian, I realise that neither preaching heresy at St Paul's Cross, nor causing scandal and brawling in Paul's nave, nor the Reformation, plagues, fires, nor even Cromwell, have destroyed the tradition of this, the only cathedral in England to be known by the name of its Saint rather than that of the city in which it stands. The encouragement of Charles II, the genius of Wren, his protégé, and the affection and generosity of the citizens of London raised the St Paul's we see today. What I had forgotten was the long sequence of ecclesiastics from AD 604 until today who have kept the Cathedral alive, even though at times in the past four centuries it may have seemed to be nearly dead.

St Paul's was not a monastic foundation, and because of this the Dean can be outvoted by the four other canons in his Chapter. 'Dr Inge once wrote that he felt like a mouse surrounded by four cats, meaning, one

St. Paul's Cathedral from the West Entrance.

fears, the residentiary canons. It is tempting to add, in Churchillian language, "Some mouse!"' Deans and Chapters are not always on good terms with their bishops. Nor are deans and canons always on good terms with one another. This history of them makes entertaining reading, and despite quarrellers, place men, pluralists and heretics there has always been someone with a genuine desire to improve the lot of the poor and teach the ignorant the Catechism.

The story includes great names – deans such as Colet, John Donne, Milman, Gregory, Church and Inge; archbishops like Bancroft, Laud and Tillotson; canons such as Sydney Smith, Liddon, Scott Holland and Alexander and minor canons like R. H. Barham, author of the *Ingoldsby Legends*. There are plenty of entertaining incidents. For instance, the amiable churchman Joseph Butler, a Georgian Dean and Bishop of Bristol in plurality, said to John Wesley: 'Sir, the pretending to extraordinary revelation and gifts of the Holy Spirit is a horrid thing, a very horrid thing.' Mendelssohn one Sunday afternoon in 1829 played the Cathedral organ for so long that the vergers, impatient to go home, persuaded the blowers to let the wind out of the instrument. Sydney Smith, complaining of the cold in the Cathedral in the winter, said: 'My sentences are frozen as they come out of my mouth and thawed in the course of the summer, making strange noises and unexpected assertions in different parts of the church.'

The successors of these wits and saints and strong personalities live today in two rows of houses at Amen Court within a stone's throw of the Cathedral. You may see them in their plane-shaded quiet if you trespass on their private road. There they are, the canons and minor canons, writing their sermons among their books. London is a cathedral city and this is its Barchester with the Dean across the road.

The last great days of St Paul's were in Victorian times, when Liddon's wonderful preaching crowded the Cathedral to capacity. But in those times a great mistake was made in the interior. The screen and organ above it, which shut off the choir from the dome and nave, were taken away. What had been a vista with mystery and a suggestion of greater riches beyond the screen became a long tunnel. Today a visitor sitting at the back of the nave could not see what is going on at the altar without a telescope, and it is very hard to pray with a telescope. Moreover, the proportions of Wren's choir were destroyed by the removal of the screen, and the new baldacchino will not improve them.

Outside, the Cathedral is unsurpassed. I do not think Wren meant the design to be seen all at once. He meant you to get glimpses down lanes and turnings. Stand in Ivy Lane, off Newgate Street, and you will see St Paul's as Wren intended. In the foreground is his restored Chapter House, coming up to the height of the bottom row of columns along the body of the building. The Victorians exceeded that height all round the

Cathedral. Our own age built Faraday House, which is the worst insult yet to St Paul's, worse even than the railway bridge at the foot of Ludgate Hill, lately made uglier by having its latticed parapet boxed in with solid panelling.

Whenever I look up from Fleet Street at the dome of Paul's and its shadowy Portland stone, bell towers and portico crowning Ludgate Hill, I am uplifted by the beauty of Wren's architecture. His 'model' design in the shape of a cross was rejected by the Dean and Chapter because they wanted a cathedral on the medieval plan with a long choir shut off from the dome and nave by a screen. Wren gave it them. St Paul's seems to me symbolic of our Church. It is a medieval plan on an ancient foundation rebuilt in the Renaissance style of its time. It is both Catholic and Reformed.

Who Will Help St Paul's?

PUNCH. 27 OCTOBER 1954

I've turned from Queen Victoria Street
   Down gas-lit lanes on windy nights
To where the wharves and water meet
   And seen the sliding river lights,
And looked through Georgian window panes
   At plasterwork in City halls
While dominant and distant reigns,
   Queen of the sky, the dome of Paul's.

Young clerks with cheeks of boyish rose
   In bars and cafés underground,
Old clerks who play at dominoes
   Where cigarette smoke hangs around,
Girl secretaries eating beans
   In restaurants with white-tiled walls —
They all know what the City means,
   They all are children of St. Paul's.

Directors who with eyes shut fast
   Are driven Esher-wards at three,
And those who leave the City last,
   Gay members of some livery
Looking in vain for cab or bus
   Down cobbled lanes where moonlight falls —
The first and last to leave of us
   Are brooded over by St. Paul's.

If in some City church we've knelt
   Shut off from traffic noise and news,
And all the past about us felt
   Among the cedar-scented pews,
Or if we think the past is rot,
   Or if our purse has other calls,
Whether we go to church or not,
   Which of us will not help St. Paul's?

Lombard Street

Words for the Lord Mayor's March

THE TIMES. 20 OCTOBER 1966

(Lady Wagner, organiser of a banquet at the Guildhall in aid of Dr Barnado's, wanted more suitable words than 'Toll for the Brave' to go with Handel's march from *Scipio* which usually plays in the Lord Mayor. John Betjeman laid down a condition that verse two must not be left out.)

Beat! drummer beat!
Heraldic trumpets blow!
By wharf and winding street
The brown Thames water flow.

The many-steepled sky
Which made our City fair,
Buried in buildings high
Is now no longer there.

But still our hearts look up
And we will take our part
In raising here the cup
To London's open heart.

Beat! drummer beat!
Let Guildhall stone resound!
When love and friendship meet
A City lost is found.

City

WHEN the great bell
    BOOMS
        Over the Portland
        stone urn,
And from the carved cedar wood
Rises the odour of incense,
    I SIT DOWN
        In St. Botolph Bishops-
        gate Churchyard
        And wait for the spirit of
        my grandfather
        Toddling along from the
        Barbican.

When I returned from school I found we'd moved:
"53 Church Street, Yes, the slummy end" —
A little laugh accompanied the joke,
For we were Chelsea now and we had friends
Whose friends had friends who knew Augustus John:
We liked bold colour schemes — orange and black —
And clever daring plays about divorce
At the St. Martin's. Oh, our lives were changed!

SUMMONED BY BELLS

At Sloane Square Station

Village on the Thames

BOOKS AND BOOKMEN. MARCH 1979

What is local is what is best. I have known Chelsea since 1917 when my parents moved to Old Church Street from Highgate. I much preferred Highgate as a place but Chelsea friends made the move congenial. How little Chelsea has changed in the last fifty years. The only thing that has ruined it is what has ruined all central London and that is the embanking of the Thames. In the Chelsea Arts Club, which is a Middlesex cottage in a large umbrageous garden, there is a painting by Napier Hemy of part of the river bank in Chelsea which conveys that Chelsea is a village on the Thames and not part of London. Admittedly, south of Harrods the Cadogan estate, in building Hans Town in red brick and a Flemish style with hints of Renaissance and much work by distinguished R A architects such as Sir Ernest George, created a new Bruges which was nothing to do with London. It now has a charm of its own and an ingenuity in the design of porches, bay windows and chimney stacks which eclipses the sunny stucco stretches of Belgravia nearer London. But Chelsea Village remains a bit of Middlesex with its much restored and historic old Church, a very Middlesex building of dark brown brick and seventeenth century in outline and proportions.

When I first came to live in Chelsea as a youth there were a lot of characters about and it was people who were more prominent than buildings. There were still people who had been patted on the head as children by Carlyle. Lawrence Street was a haunted place because of the murder at the Cross Keys Public House; Radnor Street – now Radnor Walk – was a slum; and we were told the same even in recent years, since the War, of the delightful Christchurch Street. Christ Church was very much a mission building projected from Chelsea Old Church and built on the cheap.

How well with hanseatic Hans Town went Holy Trinity Church as rebuilt in 1890 by J. D. Sedding in late Gothic freely-treated, with a riot of angels by Burne Jones in its huge east window, with electroliers in rich Edwardian swirls, with side chapels and special places for the reserved Sacrament. Holy Trinity was built High Church and attracted great crowds, and its parson's income was improved by pew rents. Today it is locked, unadvertised and unfashionable.

No building in Chelsea, and few buildings in England, are as graceful and inspiring as Wren's Royal Hospital. This long, low, stately place comes into its own entirely through the elegance of its proportions. There is not a jarring note in the long, Thames-side palace. Chapel and dining hall are joined by a stone entrance hall and the chapel, whose painted

'The Adam and Eve, Old Chelsea' by Whistler

apse has just been restored, is at its best with qualified light of day coming through clear panes onto inlaid altar piece and carved communion rails and delicate font. I know no Wren interior which satisfies me more.

Except for the Royal Hospital and Chelsea New Church (as St Luke's exuberant and paper-thin Georgian gothic is called), and always excepting Holy Trinity, Sloane Street, Chelsea has no great architecture, though there are nice little jobs by Philip Webb and housebuilders of the William Morris school of thought here and there among the genuine Queen Anne and late Georgian. Primarily it is the people who make Chelsea and of these people, artists in particular from Turner and Whistler to the present day. At no time was the Kings Road a distinguished street. Not even the vulgar new shop fronts have pulled it together. They have made it a little more like Mile End Road and Whitechapel High Street than it used to be. Frank Matcham's ebullient Chelsea Palace in orange terracotta baroque with a graceful dome has been replaced by the cheapest and ugliest shopping and residential development anywhere in London. I wish there were a photograph of the developer and his architects as well as of the beastly building with which they insulted an already drab thoroughfare. How elegant and original by contrast is the old Chelsea Town Hall by Leonard Stokes with its granite base and noble ionic porticos each designed to terminate a street vista and to pull together the intervening office building of brick and stone with a projecting clock as the central feature. I'm not sure if, next to Chelsea Hospital, the old Town Hall is not the best building left in Chelsea.

The Albert Bridge

SPECTATOR. 17 MAY 1957

I cannot believe that the London County Council decision to reconstruct the Albert Bridge, Chelsea, means that it is to be destroyed and that we will never see its graceful outline again. Shining with electric lights to show the way to Festival Gardens, or grey and airy against the London sky, it is one of the beauties of the London river and far more handsome than any of its neighbouring bridges from Westminster to Wandsworth. Its engineer, R. M. Ordish, also designed it on his patent straight-chain suspension system which he employed for the Franz Joseph bridge over the Moldau at Prague. For the Albert Bridge, which was opened in 1873, Ordish had a French engineer as partner, Le Feuvre. An original feature of the bridge is that the twenty-five-foot carriage way and eight-foot footpaths are slung between the four towers. Two years after the bridge was opened Ordish designed with Grover the roof of the Albert Hall, and in his youth he made all the working drawings for the cast iron of the Crystal Palace. I hope the LCC will make it quite clear that in any reconstruction of the bridge they are not going to destroy the towers and chains which make it the most attractive suspension bridge in London.*

*The Albert Bridge was saved.

Holy Trinity, Sloane Street

MCMVII

An acolyte singeth
Light six tapers with the Flame of Art,
Send incense wreathing to the lily flowers,
And, with your cool hands white,
Swing the warm censer round my bruised heart,
Drop, dove-grey eyes, your penitential showers
On this pale acolyte.

A cofirmandus continueth
The tall red house soars upward to the stars,
The doors are chased with sardonyx and gold,
And in the long white room
Thin drapery draws backward to unfold
Cadogan Square between the window-bars
And Whistler's mother knitting in the gloom.

The Priest endeth
How many hearts turn Motherward to-day?
(Red roses faint not on your twining stems!)
Bronze triptych doors unswing!
Wait, restive heart, wait, rounded lips, to pray,
Mid beaten copper interset with gems
Behold! Behold! your King!

A *Plea For Holy Trinity, Sloane Street*

A pamphlet illustrated by Gavin Stamp, 1974

This was one of London's most famous churches, famous for its preachers, the high quality of its music and the dignity of its ritual. It was much used in the days before people went out of London for Saturday and Sunday. It was built in 1888–90 in a free style of Gothic from the designs of John Dando Sedding, a Master of the Art Workers' Guild, a friend of William Morris, Edward Burne-Jones, John Ruskin and Norman Shaw. Sedding believed that a church should be 'wrought and painted over with everything that has life and beauty – in frank and fearless naturalism covered with men and beasts and flowers'. 'I do congratulate you on your new church,' wrote Norman Shaw to Sedding, 'What arches! What surprises! I see that great East Window filled with little angels, shall we not call Morris in on this – the wisest of men on such occasions?'

The result was that Holy Trinity is a celebration of the Arts and Crafts Movement. It only lacks a Bishop's Throne to be the Cathedral of West London, for its nave is wider than that of St Paul's (– by 9″!). It abounds in side altars and chapels for occasional services. Harry Wilson, Sedding's successor after his early death in 1891, designed the pulpit and the beaten metal screens. A notable feature of the church was the electroliers by Starkie Gardner. The stained-glass, apart from Burne-Jones' East Window, is by Christopher Whall, the artist of the windows in the Lady Chapel of Gloucester Cathedral, and Sir William Richmond. Sculptors such as Armstead, Pomeroy, Sir Hamo Thorneycroft and Onslow Ford carved for the church.

After a long period of thought and prayer, the Rector and congregation have decided that there is no way of retaining the present building as a centre of worship except by pulling it down and building a new church. Unless something is done, Sedding's irreplaceable church and the works of art designed especially for it will be destroyed for ever and dispersed.*

*Sedding's church was not destroyed.

[69]

Holy Trinity, Sloane Street

SUNDAY TIMES. 15 SEPTEMBER 1974

Bishop, archdeacon, rector, wardens, mayor
Guardians of Chelsea's noblest house of prayer,

You who your church's vastness deplore
"Should we not sell and give it to the poor?"

Recall, despite your practical suggestion
Which the disciple was who asked that question.

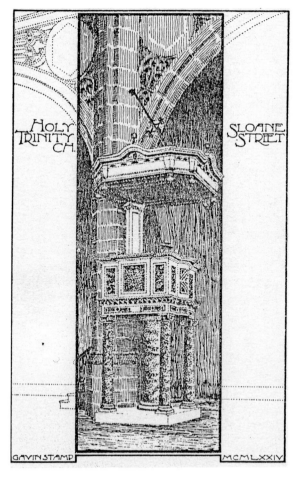

Chelsea 1977

The street is bathed in winter sunset pink,
The air is redolent of kitchen sink,
Between the dog-mess heaps I pick my way
To watch the dying embers of the day
Glow over Chelsea, crimson load on load
All Brangwynesque across the long King's Road.
Deep in myself I feel a sense of doom,
Fearful of death I trudge towards the tomb.
The earth beneath my feet is hardly soil
But outstretched chicken-netting coil on coil
Covering cables, sewage-pipes and wires
While underneath burn hell's eternal fires.
Snap, crackle! pop! the kiddiz know the sound
And Satan stokes his furnace underground.

Radnor Walk, Chelsea

[71]

MIDDLESEX

The expeditions by North London trains
To dim forgotten stations, wooden shacks
On oil-lit flimsy platforms among fields
As yet unbuilt-on, deep in Middlesex . . .

SUMMONED BY BELLS

Outside Norman Shaw's Grimsdyke at Harrow

Ah Middlesex

PUNCH. 14 APRIL 1954

Even more surely than civics, eurhythmics, art-history and other delightful things, our buildings say to us: 'We once were civilized. We are so no more.'

Consider Middlesex, that most hardly used of all counties. I hear in my mind's ear, and it is no fantasy, the Middlesex of forty years ago. I hear the clink of a smithy at Stanwell, the clap-to of a tollgate in Hampstead Lane, the creak of rowlocks at Shepperton, the jingle of harness in Hammersmith, the buzz of flies rising from shops in Chiswick High Road where goods lie open to the public way. I hear the hiss and grind of a London United Electrical Tramcar, majestic in its cream and royal blue, through Twickenham. I hear the thud of a pair of carthorses and the creaking rumble of an enormous wagon passing down the rich flat market-garden land from Harmondsworth to West Drayton; in the airy heights of Stanmore and along the oak-paled lanes of Enfield Chase glistening carriages go spanking round corners, and I hear them crunch over a gravelled drive which leads between conifers and private lamp-posts to some city merchant's red-brick mansion. And here and there all over this still countrified county a row of grey brick houses, a coal-merchant's, an estate agent's and a sweet-shop mark the road to a railway station, and I hear the puffing of a tank engine drawing its load of clerks into the fields from the prison of the city.

Ripe for development, one fears

This Georgian bow-fronted shop-front has somehow survived in Brentford High Street, where it is all the better for being a real shop and not a dead thing, stuck up in a museum. Because it is the product of thoughtful and honest craftsmanship, it still looks beautiful and in keeping with its setting.

[73]

In my mind's nose I smell straw and stables and leather and saddle-soap and dried horse-dung and dried cow-dung, and then come waves of bean scent. And in spring that most prevalent of all Middlesex blossoms, the may, whitening uneven hedges, and here and there turning faintly pink, sends its scent as far into London as Kensington and Hornsey. On the trams there is a smell of metal polish where brass has been rubbed up for the day; in the steam trains a smell of sulphur and dry upholstery. In the new-fangled electric trains rattling out to recent red-brick development in Acton, Willesden and Neasden the more familiar smell of pipe-smoke and other people. And from a country inn, weather-boarded and with swinging sign, comes the rich smell of strong beer.

In my mind's eye I see dark cedars behind garden walls of brown and red, orange and gold Middlesex brick, the most beautiful brick in England. I see wisteria climbing over a pale Georgian house-front and mulberries shadowing white wood gates. I see great elms on little hills, ducks floating on the cressy Brent, and more ducks on village pond and hens scratching the dusty road from Ruislip to Ickenham. I see a pair of wooden cottages for land workers and great timbered barns whose boards are tarred with black and whose roofs, like all Middlesex roofs, are warmly tiled in red.

Old Middlesex, the vegetable garden and dairy farm of London, where are you now? Where are the merchants' houses with their walled gardens, miniature landscaped parks, little lakes and carriage drives and bridges?

We went to Brentford, Fougasse and I, which is now the capital of Middlesex, seeing that the upstart London has taken Westminster and many a delightful parish from the county. We went to what is left of Brentford, for a ruthless local council has destroyed much of its narrow High Street and jammed ill-proportioned, bogusly-simple 'modern'

This, the Great Worst Road, is within a mile of Brentford's High Street. Notice the 'artistic' hoarding on the left, built to look like a magnified modernistic fireplace. You cannot see the antirrhinums and floodlights which adorn its little garden in front and turn it into an 'amenity'. But you can see the motor cars beyond, and beyond again, the 'sprinkling of light industry', whose pseudo-modern outlines assault your eye. Is it two o'clock as it tells us it is on the neo-Egyptian building, or five past four as it says on the right-hand packing case? No matter. We are outside time here and in the great new technical civilization of tomorrow – and, alas, today.

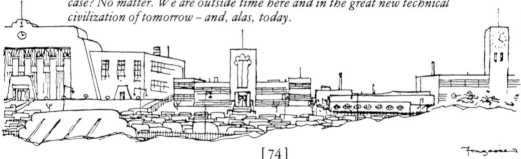

buildings among the older houses. After the first asphyxiating minutes by the gasworks we still found bits of old Middlesex in Brentford.

Then we went northward to the Great Worst Road where it is bordered by what the planners call 'a sprinkling of light industry'. The hooting of neurotics in saloon cars, the bullying thunder of lorries, sirens summoning workers to canteens, the treacly swoop through walls of glass of 'Music While You Work' and, loud above the lot, the roar of aeroplanes assailed our ears.

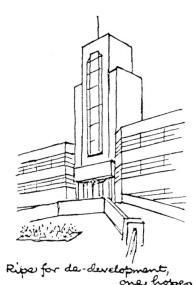

The person who designed this factory front must have had a great antipathy to curves. Once this sort of thing, which came to us from America and the Continent, was thought to show 'clean modern lines'. Today it seems to show a plethora of awkward angles. It will never weather. But it will always look unbeautiful and has long looked out of date.

Ripe for de-development, one hopes

Petrol, diesel oil and antiseptic assailed our nostrils, and from certain factories came the whiff of synthetic scent which makes one's thoughts fly, light as plastic, to saloons with 'clean modern lines', paper flowers sprouting from clean modern vases fixed to walls, unemptied ash-trays and everything washable.

And what chance strokes of some raw architectural student using a 2B pencil and remembering vaguely some Continental magazine of twenty years ago created this neo-Egyptian, neo-jazz world of factories? How many wires and poles and pipes must cross our delicate landscape to these hard-shaped buildings with their pseudo-simple angles and pathetic landscape gardens studded with snapdragons and floodlights? Warm air-conditioned world of beige and cream! Safe, labour-saving world of buff-tiled fireplaces, television sets and football pools! Hygienic world of community centres and culture, but not too much of it! There is no birth. There is no death. We will all go on for ever and ever getting better and better. Break in, O bells of Brentford, from your fifteenth-century tower to remind us of the Truth.

[75]

Middlesex

Gaily into Ruislip Gardens
   Runs the red electric train,
With a thousand Ta's and Pardon's
   Daintily alights Elaine;
Hurries down the concrete station
With a frown of concentration,
Out into the outskirt's edges
Where a few surviving hedges
Keep alive our lost Elysium — rural Middlesex again.

Well cut Windsmoor flapping lightly,
   Jacqmar scarf of mauve and green
Hiding hair which, Friday nightly,
   Delicately drowns in Drene;
Fair Elaine the bobby-soxer,
Fresh-complexioned with Innoxa,
Gains the garden — father's hobby —
Hangs her Windsmoor in the lobby,
Settles down to sandwich supper and the television screen.

Gentle Brent, I used to know you
   Wandering Wembley-wards at will,
Now what change your waters show you
   In the meadowlands you fill!
Recollect the elm-trees misty
And the footpaths climbing twisty
Under cedar-shaded palings,
Low laburnum-leaned-on railings,
Out of Northolt on and upward to the heights of Harrow hill.

Parish of enormous hayfields
   Perivale stood all alone,
And from Greenford scent of mayfields
   Most enticingly was blown
Over market gardens tidy,
Taverns for the *bona fide*,
Cockney anglers, cockney shooters,
Murray Poshes, Lupin Pooters
Long in Kensal Green and Highgate silent under soot and stone.

Tottenham

TELEGRAPH WEEKEND MAGAZINE. 6 JULY 1973

A slight sense of country comes as soon as you get out of the Victoria Line at Seven Sisters. You can even feel it on the Great Eastern, after the train has climbed from Liverpool Street and is passing above the chimney pots through Hackney Downs and Rectory Road and Stamford Hill, on its way to Enfield. Out on the pavement of the Tottenham High Road there is more width. Side roads are broader, skies are wider. Trees may be seen in back gardens.

Here and there are handsome brick houses of the 18th century. The dentist and the doctor inhabit a splendid pair. Their front gardens have not yet been built over by shops. We are in the valley of the Lea and going north. William Morris, before he became craftsman and socialist, spent his childhood at Walthamstow. 'What with the beasts and the men, and the scattered red-tiled roofs, and the big hayricks,' he wrote, 'it does not make a bad holiday to get a quiet pony and ride about there on a sunny afternoon of Autumn, and look over the river and the craft passing up and down, and on to Shooter's Hill and the Kentish uplands, and then turn round to the wide green sea of the Essex marshland, with the great domed line of the sky, and the sun shining down in one flood of peaceful light . . . To this day when I smell a May-tree, I think of going to bed by daylight.'

If London is still a collection of villages, except for the City and Westminster – and I think it is – then Tottenham on the Middlesex bank of the Lea next to Walthamstow, is one of the most attractive and village-like. To the east, across the wide marshes and sports grounds and reservoirs of the River Lea, are the tree-clad heights of Epping Forest. To the west the wooded slopes of Hornsey and Highgate are higher and nearer. Always on the western skyline is an unexpected view of the Alexandra Palace, curved in the middle, with projections at either end. Now when people think of Tottenham, which was the next parish to Morris, they think of football and the Spurs.

Tottenham was not so smart a Middlesex village as Twickenham or Chiswick in the 18th century, and this despite the fact that the Smithsons owned the east of the parish. One of them had married the heiress of the Percy family, and was created Duke of Northumberland in 1766. Their domain in Tottenham included water mills and Tottenham marshes, which were famous for cowslips and large-flowered forget-me-nots. The peerage is recalled in the road and railway station, Northumberland Park. On the marshes the Tottenham Hotspur football team played when they were first founded in 1882 out of a cricket team. The Hotspur is a reference to Harry Hotspur, the Earl of Northumberland, in Shakespeare's *Henry IV*, *part II*.

Besides being known for sport and wild flowers, Tottenham was famous for bricks and tiles. The earth here was baked into beautiful dark bricks from the Middle Ages until 1961. Old walls that survive in Tottenham are worth looking at; you can find them in back gardens, between houses off the High Road, and in passages and in the older houses. They vary from shiny black, through dark red and light red and brown, to pale pink, yellow and grey. On the whole, the smaller they are, the older they are.

Tottenham was also famous in the 18th century for Quakers, whose meeting house, founded in 1680, survives, though completely rebuilt, off the High Road. The Quakers kept schools in the parish. These were not Squeers-like establishments – though strict they were calm and ordered. Looking at some of those handsome, late-Georgian, square houses that may be seen behind the shops and traffic of the High Road and White Hart Lane, it is easy to imagine that they once had trim front gardens, and an orchard and a paddock at the back, and a large room on the ground floor, through whose window panes the school children looked despairingly out on to the Middlesex sky.

The Quakers were the chief tradesmen of Tottenham too. In 1909 Mrs Couchman wrote a fascinating book of Reminiscences of early Victorian Tottenham. She remembered the apothecary's shop, with its row of coloured bottles, next to the Friends' Meeting House. One day 'Mr Thomas Shillitoe, one of the Society of Friends, opened a Chemist's shop next door. He had what I considered a very objectionable habit. When pouring out medicine he always licked the last drop from the bottle.'

An Anglican clergyman and artist lived in a big house where the police station stood later. He was the Reverend Thomas Powell. 'He had a large garden with bathroom and swimming bath in the middle of the lawn, all beautifully tiled; at the back there was a fish pond and meadow. The last time I saw him he was looking over the high brick wall with a blanket over his shoulders. He used to give dinner parties to his gentlemen friends; everything prepared and sent down with waiters from London.

'I think Mr Powell must have been particularly fond of violets, they grew in his garden in such profusion.'

In 1843 the railway from Liverpool Street opened a station at Tottenham and another at Northumberland Park. The farms beside the marshes were soon built over with grey brick houses. In the 1870s another line from Liverpool Street came nearer to old Tottenham, on its way to Enfield, and the Midland Railway ran a line from St Pancras. There was hardly a field left. By this time the houses were of red brick, most of them two-storey. In the present century Tottenham has become

The Priory

the Birmingham of London, that is to say, a large and varied collection of light industries, whose sheds extend over what once were back gardens and orchards, leaving here and there small municipal parks. It is hard to imagine there was ever any country here at all.

Yet the effect of the village of Tottenham survives. If you walk up Bruce Grove, which climbs a straight incline from Tottenham High Road, it is easy to imagine that this may once have been a broad avenue of elms or oaks leading to a country house. At the top of the incline you realise you are right. For there, terminating Bruce Grove, is Bruce Castle. Its old brick walls and central clock tower rise above shrubs and a brown brick garden wall and a cedar-planted park. What you are looking at is a 17th-century house largely refaced in the early 18th century. Beside it is a curious conical brick structure, resembling a folly, and dating from the 16th century.

Bruce Castle is now the central office of the libraries, museum and arts department of the Borough of Haringey. The castle was saved from destruction through the efforts of the now defunct Borough of Tottenham. In the last century the castle was used as a school, one of whose earliest masters was Rowland Hill, inventor of the penny post. Before that it was inhabited by private persons, notably a Lord Coleraine. And in the Middle Ages there stood a castle here which belonged to the Bruces, the family of King Robert Bruce. Edward II confiscated it from them in 1306, because Robert Bruce had joined the forces against England.

When you walk out into the park of the castle, near the children's swings and playground, a shapely spreading oak tree reminds you that this is clay soil and good for bricks. And there, beyond the castle park, is a 17th-century brick house, the Priory. It was a farm within living memory. It is now the vicarage, and entered by splendid 18th-century iron gates. In one of the rooms in front there is a Jacobean ceiling of moulded plaster-work, and an elaborate carved wooden chimneypiece in the best 18th-century style, better really than the chimney pieces in Bruce Castle itself.

Next to the Priory is the Church of All Hallows – the London name for All Saints. The Church is surprising, varied and beautiful. Outside the old flint tower is very roughly built, and topped with 18th-century bricks. It has a village look. Stone walls are on the south side, which once must have been plastered. Also on the south side is a handsome Tudor porch, with a room above. The walls of this porch are of local dark red brick, patterned over in diamonds with black bricks. In the churchyard are grand 18th-century tombs of Portland stone, obelisks and table tombs, some with iron railings round them. Because a public footpath goes through the churchyard (lit with hideous concrete lamp standards like thick button hooks) finely carved stones have been smashed up by vandals. Each of these tombs must once have stood for the family of some rich City merchant, who had set himself up as a minor squire in the parish, with a

All Hallows Church

comfortable square Georgian house, and a walled garden, and some pear trees. Because of vandals the church has now to be kept locked at all times.

The east end of the church is a harsh contrast with the rest of this village building, it is of red brick with black diaper pattern over it, and was supposed, by its architect, William Butterfield, to match the brick work of the Tudor porch. Butterfield was a great friend of a former Vicar of Tottenham, Canon Hall, and he has made the interior of Tottenham church one of the most uplifting and stately in Middlesex. He gave to this little country church a huge and harmoniously painted wooden roof and clerestory, and a rich chancel full of coloured marbles and a font to match. The west window of the north aisle of All Hallows is filled with stained glass of about 1590. So good is Butterfield's enlargement of the church, from the inside at any rate, that this old glass is not put out of countenance by his violent colour schemes. He is buried in the cemetery a little way along on the right of the path to the north of the Church, alongside his friend Canon Hall.

To complete the village effect, near the church there is an Inn, The Antwerp Arms. From its back garden and over its fence you can see a row of Middlesex cottages with curly red tiles and tall red chimney pots on dark brown-brick stacks.* They back on to another charming row of houses called Prospect Place. Stand in the cemetery and look towards the church or stand in the road outside the Priory and look towards the Antwerp Arms, or stand in the park of Bruce Castle and look at the whole group – and you will see the England of Constable and Cotman. It will not be there much longer unless the Borough of Haringey can protect the churchyard, which it now owns, and has the foresight to keep standing the old cottages of Tottenham. It will be cheaper and kinder to repair and enlarge these little houses, than to destroy and build again.

*The 'row of Middlesex cottages' are in Cemetery Road. They have been bought and restored by Haringey Council.

Mount Avenue, Ealing, 1902

Lines written to Martyn Skinner before his Departure from Oxfordshire in Search of Quiet – 1961

Return, return to Ealing,
   Worn poet of the farm!
Regain your boyhood feeling
   Of uninvaded calm!
For there the leafy avenues
   Of lime and chestnut mix'd
Do widely wind, by art designed,
   The costly houses 'twixt.

No early morning tractors
   The thrush and blackbird drown,
No nuclear reactors
   Bulge huge below the down,
No youth upon his motor-bike
   His lust for power fulfils,
With dentist's drill intent to kill
   The silence of the hills.

In Ealing on a Sunday
   Bell-haunted quiet falls,
In Ealing on a Monday
   'Milk-o!' the milkman calls;
No lorries grind in bottom gear
   Up steep and narrow lanes,
Nor constant here offend the ear
   Low-flying aeroplanes.

Return, return to Ealing,
   Worn poet of the farm!
Regain your boyhood feeling
   Of uninvaded calm!
Where smoothly glides the bicycle
   And softly flows the Brent
And a gentle gale from Perivale
   Sends up the hayfield scent.

Syon House

Broadcast on the Home Service of the BBC in May 1952

I should not think that anywhere in England there is a richer two-and-sixpence worth than in a visit to Syon House, Middlesex. Next to Hampton Court it is the finest thing in the county. And it has the advantage over Hampton Court of still being lived in by the family. It is not a dead museum but a living house. The Duke of Northumberland keeps it as a country place. There are two hundred and sixty acres of country around it, yet it is within twenty minutes of Hammersmith Broadway – two hundred and sixty acres of meadows with fat cattle, lime avenues, rare trees, lakes and walled gardens, all on the Middlesex bank of the Thames opposite Kew. And before we enter Syon, remember Middlesex, for it is all round us here. Dear Middlesex, a century and a half ago the most beautiful county in England with its cedar-shaded lawns, brown brick walls, little hills and mighty elms hiding the country retreats of London merchants and the weather-boarded cottages of their retainers. Then that greedy upstart the County of London raped many square miles of it and stole the City of Westminster which was its capital.

Brentford is now the capital of Middlesex – Brentford 'For dirty streets and white-legged chickens famed' as the poet Gay described it in Queen Anne's time – and it is by Brentford that we approach Syon House from London. First there is a fearful smell of gas, and then the long winding High Street of this ancient town. It has some Georgian shop fronts, many old Middlesex houses with their hipped roofs and uneven tiles, glimpses of the river between wharves and a tempting Georgian church which is always locked. Brentford should paint its old houses and repair them. It is ashamed of itself and has no need to be for it has charming features under a dirty face, and I hope the 'progressive' planners will preserve it and not do the old reactionary thing of pulling it down.

Now let us go down the old coaching road to the west, and there on the left are the entrance gates of Syon. They are a rich colonnade with the gates in the middle and the statue of a lion over the top – the lion is the crest of the Percys, the Dukes of Northumberland. You'll see the idea of these gates – they are not fierce portcullis-like things to keep you out. No, Robert Adam meant them as an airy screen to act as a frame through which you can see the cool green park from the dusty high road. They were built to please the passing traveller, not to intimidate him. Even so, you cannot see the house from them, only acres of meadow.

We don't enter the park by these gates, but between old garden walls nearer Brentford or round at the exquisite Thames-side village of

[86]

Isleworth which I shall mention at the end of this talk. And as we walk through these meadows, let me tell you of some of the thrilling history of the house. For centuries it has been associated with blood and executions. Henry V founded Syon Convent to atone for his father's sin of murdering Richard II. Henry VIII locked up his Queen Catherine Howard here before sending her to the block. Henry VIII's own coffin burst open here in the night and dogs licked the King's blood. Protector Somerset was executed after living here. So was Lady Jane Grey. Guy Fawkes rode out from Syon to blow up Parliament. Our Royal Martyr Charles I rode over here to see his children, a day or two before his execution.

Let us glide into the more comfortable reign of George III. A Yorkshire baronet had married the last lady with much of the original Percy blood, and took the name and arms of Percy. He was eventually made first Duke of Northumberland. He was a good businessman and – unusual combination, but not so unusual in those days – he was also a man of taste. He employed Robert Adam to redesign the interior of Syon in 1762. He employed the great landscape artist Lancelot 'Capability' Brown to lay out the park. Brown said that nature abhorred a straight line, so he cut down most of the straight clipped avenues and created winding vistas with clumps of mighty trees. He dammed a little tributary of the Brent called the Brent Bourne which ran through the park, and turned it into two lakes. These were spanned by elegant cast-iron bridges.

And there, glimpsed through one of Capability's winding vistas, we can at last see the house. You will say at first, how disappointing, what a barrack of a place! For it is very plain outside. Like all good English things, its beauty is not on the surface. What we see is just a big square house, three storeys high with towers at the corners. It is all very plain and was faced with Bath stone in George IV's reign. Not an ornament. All the glory is within. Any outward glory is provided by Nature tamed by man in the rolling park. It is a luxuriant contrast to the plainness of the house, an intentional contrast.

Come now to the entrance porch and pull that ducal bell in its brazen socket. Wires must run down miles of passages to some remote basement where fifty labelled bells bear the names of fifty different parts of the house. You and I are going to see the best of the house, for the Duke and his family live in lesser rooms whose windows look on to the central court-yard of Syon, which is like the court of an unimportant Cambridge college. They have left the most exciting part of the house for us to see.

The front door opens and here we are in the Great Hall, square at one end, rounded at the other. All is white and cool. The plaster work of the ceiling is echoed in the black and white marble of the floor. Statues of Roman heroes stand on pedestals designed by Robert Adam. We are in for a triumphal progress, going from beauty to greater beauty round the house. What is architecture? I wish I could tell you in a few words. But it is here at Syon. It is something to do with proportion and colour and light and shade. It adds to the dignity of man. This place makes you feel like a king as you walk through its Georgian perfection, through this wonderful series of rooms, designed by Robert Adam – furniture, plaster-work, floors and all – for the delight of eye and heart.

Look to your right. Over that bronze statue of the Dying Gaul you see the Ante-Room. There are twelve green marble columns round it; their capitals are gold and above them are gold statues; the ceiling is gilded, the walls are pale green, the floor is of coloured scagliogla marble, and in the middle of the room is a gilded Sèvres vase which is as big as a bath tub. By a clever device which you don't see at once, this rich ante-room seems to be square though it is really oblong.

Now we are well upon the principal floor and can look out on the park. Not a house is in sight. Game, wild duck and herons abound. Trees stand heavy with shadow, emerald where the sun strikes them. And now we come to the dining room with columns and semi-domes at either end, and white statues in dark red niches down the side. When I was there last, they set its clock going. It was made by Vulliamy the famous clock maker in about 1785. At the hour, it plays a woodwind organ which sends fluting notes like bird song down these elegant spaces. Wherever the eye rests, on mouldings, furniture, fabrics, there is elegance and craftsmanship. I am reminded of Siegfried Sassoon's splendid phrase: 'long-apprenticed, unpresuming skill'. It is everywhere around – in the gilded lead mouldings laid on ivory round the doors, in the mahogany doors themselves, in the chairs and tables and carpets and light fittings and chimney pieces – all designed by Robert Adam and executed by the best Georgian craftsmen and artists. Here indeed was civilisation.

The next room is a great contrast. It is the red drawing room. After the pale creams and pinks of the dining room, it is a riot of scarlet and gold. The walls are hung with Spitalfields silk in scarlet, the domed ceiling is adorned with red and blue medallions in gilt frames. The floor has a carpet made at Moorfields in the City of London in greens and pinks and blues from an Adam design, the chimney piece is decorated with ormolu. On the walls hang portraits by Lely and Van Dyck of Royal people associated with the house – Henrietta Maria and Charles I and their children.

We conclude this triumphal progress with what is to me the most beautiful room of all, the Gallery. It runs along the whole river length of the house. It is the Elizabethan long gallery where Cromwell once walked, redecorated by Adam. Carpet, furniture, colouring is just as Robert Adam left it. The ceiling is lilac and gold. One wall is all bookshelves with pale green pilasters between them and painted scenes above. The brown leather of the books looks like pale autumn leaves in all this greenness. Another wall is all windows. For the perfection of its proportion – the way it just escapes being a passage and becomes a long diminishing room – this gallery is I think the climax of the walk. For architecture is, above everything, proportion.

Outside the house once more, you can have tea in the hay-scented riding school, and walk to the flower garden where there is a domed conservatory designed by the great Charles Fowler, architect of Covent Garden Market. At Syon he has constructed a St Paul's Cathedral dome of glass. Beyond it is a lake with rare trees including a deciduous cypress which normally grows in swamps and whose breather roots stick out of the ground all round it like gigantic upturned turnips. The earth at Syon is even richer than Kew's and has been put to as good use.

But architecture is civilisation's strongest memorial. Syon is a memorial of a peak of our civilisation, the Georgian era when 'Rule Britannia' was composed, money poured in, artists and writers gave of their best, unfrustrated and encouraged by great patrons.

At the western end of Syon is the little Georgian village of Isleworth with its walled gardens, its tumbling weir, its Georgian houses and its old church. After the war, after all the attempted havoc by bombs and doodle-bugs – sixty-nine bombs fell in Syon's grounds and two went through the roof – after all that damage by the Nazis, there came a little gang of English boys who burned down Isleworth church. And since the war the decoration of James Wyatt's elegant pavilion on the river bank was defaced, though it is now being rebuilt. When I walked with the owner in an empty part of the park near the old cockpit, we found a garden tap had been torn up in an attempt to steal its lead piping. We live in an age of vandalism. We destroy our craftsmanship. Go and see Syon while it is still there. It is not an escape. It is an inspiration.

Harrow School Songs

THE LISTENER. 17 JANUARY 1974

E. E. Bowen and John Farmer started the collection of Harrow School Songs, in the 1870s. I first became aware of these marvellous songs during childhood rambles in rural Middlesex – my lost Elysium. Outside these, there's no great tradition of music at Harrow. The music schools are perched dankly on a steep, north-facing slope on the way to the football fields, and before Farmer's time there was fearful hostility to the earliest efforts to form a Musical Society. Farmer broke through by gradually persuading house-masters to allow weekly glee-singing in the winter months in the various houses of the school. Those boys who couldn't sing didn't just 'la-la': they said the words, and they were called 'Talking Josephs'. The boys who really could sing were called 'Canaries', and, oh! dear me, what does that rhyme with? Believe it or not, one of the Bowen/Farmer songs is called 'Fairies':

> O'er twenty leagues of morning dew,
>   Across the cheery breezes,
> Can fairies fail to whisper true
>   What youth and fancy pleases?
> As strength decays with after days,
>   And eyes have ceased to glisten,
> Those souls alone not older grown
>   Will have the ears to listen.
> Keep youth a guest of heart and breast,
>   And though the hair be whiter —
> Ho, ho! Ha, ha! Tra la la la!
>   You hear them all the brighter!

The old school-building looks Elizabethan, and originally it was. But in 1821 the correct but brilliant architect Cockerell enlarged it and gave it symmetry between a pair of crow-stepped gables. By his skill, the building you see today still looks like an ancient grammar school on top of a hill with a more or less flat yard in front of it, where the roll-call known as 'Bill' takes place. There's a song which celebrates this ritual, when each boy in his appointed order queues up, files past the beak and answers, 'Here sir', as his name is called:

> Here Sir! Here Sir! Here Sir! Here Sir!
>   On the top of Harrow Hill,
> Here Sir! Here Sir! Here Sir! Here Sir!
>   In the windy yard at Bill.

'Here Sir!' (1888) was written by Edmund Whytehead Howson, with music by Eaton Faning. And so was another song, a waltz tune called 'Ducker' – the open-air swimming-pool across the fields and surrounded by a belt of trees, where boys were not allowed to wear anything in the water, but on land strolled about wearing enormous towels like huge togas and munching Ducker buns about twelve inches across. Now, because of the encroachments of Kenton and the admission of women, trunks are the rule. Thank God the song hasn't changed:

> O the joy of being idle
>   And heroically slack!
> Would you always wear a bridle
>   With a burden on your back?
> Truce awhile to toil and tasking,
>   Dream away the hours with us,
> With a bun and towel basking
>   *Puris naturalibus!*

The same partnership, Howson and Faning, contributed a song of heraldic inspiration. The school's motto is *Stet Fortuna Domus*: 'May the good fortune of this house stand.' The song with that title is especially marked out, because in 1943 an extra verse was added to signify Winston Churchill's visit to the school to hear the singing. He was an even worse scholar of the school than Byron, but every year from 1940 he came to the performance of what have become known as the 'Churchill Songs'. I'm told he wept buckets. Here's the new Churchill verse:

> Nor less we praise in sterner days
>   The leader of our nation,
> And Churchill's name shall win acclaim
>   From each new generation.
> While in this fight to guard the Right
>   Our country you defend, Sir,
> Here grim and gay we mean to stay,
>   And stick it to the end, Sir.

The last song I'll mention is 'The Silver Arrow'. At one time, archery was a compulsory activity at Harrow and the winner's prize was a silver arrow. This song was written in 1910 by C. J. Maltby, with music by Sir Percy Buck:

> The book is read and the prayers are said,
>   Then all to the butts repair,
> The men are seen in the jerkin green,
>   And the maidens are watching there.
> Full well they know no foreign foe
>   Our shores will dare invade,
> With pikemen bold our walls to hold,
>   And archers in every glade.

Harrow-on-the-Hill

When melancholy Autumn comes to Wembley
    And electric trains are lighted after tea
The poplars near the Stadium are trembly
    With their tap and tap and whispering to me,
        Like the sound of little breakers
        Spreading out along the surf-line
When the estuary's filling
        With the sea.

Then Harrow-on-the-Hill's a rocky island
    And Harrow churchyard full of sailors' graves
And the constant click and kissing of the trolley buses hissing
    Is the level to the Wealdstone turned to waves
        And the rumble of the railway
        Is the thunder of the rollers
As they gather up for plunging
        Into caves.

There's a storm cloud to the westward over Kenton,
    There's a line of harbour lights at Perivale,
Is it rounding rough Pentire in a flood of sunset fire
    The little fleet of trawlers under sail?
        Can those boats be only roof tops
        As they stream along the skyline
In a race for port and Padstow
        With the gale?

Harrow Hill

RAILWAYS AND THE UNDERGROUND

Great was our joy, Ronald Hughes Wrights's and mine,
To travel by the Underground all day
Between the rush hours, so that very soon
There was no station, north to Finsbury Park,
To Barking eastwards, Clapham Common south,
No temporary platform in the west
Among the Actons and the Ealings, where
We had not once alighted . . .
We knew the different railways by their smells.
The City and South reeked like a changing-room
Its orange engines and old rolling-stock,
Its narrow platforms, undulating tracks,
Seemed even then historic. Next in age,
The Central London, with its cut-glass shades
On draughty stations, had an ozone smell —
Not seaweed-scented ozone from the sea
But something chemical from Birmingham.
                    SUMMONED BY BELLS

Euston

ARCHITECTURAL REVIEW. SEPTEMBER 1933

For many years now there have been rumours about the reconstruction of Euston, the demolition of its great arch and its old booking hall, now known as the Great Hall.

The London and Birmingham Railway, inaugurated in 1836, reached the Metropolis in 1838. It was an early railway to arrive. The Directors, aware of the important architectural and engineering qualities of their undertaking, employed the best architect of the time to construct their stations, approaches and bridges. Philip Hardwick had indeed shown far-reaching powers as an architect, erecting both commercial and monumental buildings in the best contemporary manner. He became official architect of the Birmingham Railway in 1836 and designed the gigantic Ionic station for Birmingham, and completed Euston Grove in 1838. Now only the great arch remains of his original design for Euston, all but one of its lodges have been swept away, the ironwork has been displaced and that fine entrance has lost the significance it had when it acted as a foreground to the tree-clad hills of Hampstead and Highgate behind. In 1841 Euston Square was built at a distance great enough to allow Philip Hardwick's superb piece of decorative architecture to remain untroubled. In 1847 Philip Hardwick's son, Philip C. Hardwick (1820–92), who had been up till 1840 in Blore's office, helped his father to complete the Great Hall as an addition to the old station. The influence of the father may be set down in the general massiveness of the structure and in its powerful simplicity; the son no doubt contributing Roman details and indeed a Roman air to the whole thing, out of keeping with, though no less successful than, his father's great arch.

When P. C. Hardwick worked alone, as at the Great Western Hotel, Paddington, and in his baroque design for an Albert Memorial, he displayed the elaborate taste of his age. Towards the end of his professional career he found classical architecture did not pay, and allowed the Elizabethan influence of Blore to get the better of the Greek influence of his father. He built Charterhouse School, Lambeth Church, Wandsworth Freemasons' School, in sugary Gothic and Tudor. Therefore, when he came later in life to put some rather hurried additions on to Euston, though respecting the classical style of the old station, he belittled its former grandeur with mean and French extensions. Since his death, the

The Great Hall

[99]

Company's architects cannot be said to have improved its general appearance. The last indignity which Euston has suffered is the erection of a kiosk in a restrained jazz-modern style in the Great Hall. You can have tea in this hall during the summer months, and little baskets of artificial flowers are hung from Hardwick's noble balcony.

Obviously something must be done for Euston: it is almost, although it can never be quite, as impracticable as are Waterloo, Victoria, Cannon Street, Charing Cross, Fenchurch Street, Liverpool Street and London Bridge. But whatever is done let it not be done in the all too familiar railway manner. If the Directors of the L.M.S. decide to rebuild Euston let us hope they will make a clean sweep of the building behind the Doric portico, and employ outside advice and assistance. As has been shown already, a new Euston is not a matter to be decided by old gentlemen in the mahogany confines of Hardwick's imposing Boardroom. Nevertheless the Directors of the L.M.S. have made one splendid gesture in sanctioning the erection of a first-rate piece of architecture in the form of the Morecambe Hotel. If their public spirit and enterprise have allowed them to do this for Morecambe, how much more should they do for London? The first duty of the Directors is to employ a good architect who will not ruin an excellent chance of the improvement of London, as did the London and South-Western when it created that mean and ostentatious building, Waterloo. Let the L.M.S. employ what is publicly known as a 'proper architect' (not necessarily a knighted one). Next let them submit all the plans and elevations to a Committee of Judges.

If in these new schemes the Great Hall must go, then that is that, and if the arch must be abolished, then that is that too.* But at least this splendid gateway should be re-erected in another place where it would be not only an excellent advertisement but also a permanent and impressive memorial of the once great architectural tradition of the railways.

*The Arch and Great Hall were destroyed in 1963.

[101]

Nooks and Corners

PRIVATE EYE. 10 SEPTEMBER 1971

Why not spend your holidays at the lovely new Euston this year?

After an invigorating uphill climb from the platform to the air-conditioned Main Circulating Area, you will be dazzled by the variety of choices. The hall itself is so magnificent with its two supporting columns that we were tempted to show it in our illustration. But as it hardly exists, except as air, a deliciously conditioned mixture of sweat and deodorants, there seemed no need to photograph it.

Many choices are offered – paperbacks, cafeteria, warmed alcohol and souvenirs. Those in a hurry will want to join the taxi queue, or the almost equally long queue to the underground. If you like fresh air, then the best you will find comes up from the moving stairs on the underground. More sophisticated tourists will enjoy the diesel-scented corridors leading down to the taxi rank. Let us suppose you have time to 'stand and stare'. Stand you most certainly will. There are sixteen plastic seats round the columns, and we must think of the old folk and the kiddies first, mustn't we?

Well the first thing that will strike you will be the two significant mono-liths which symbolise the new Euston. They are on a site in front of the station which would have provided ample room for the old-fashioned Doric Propylaeum, designed in 1836 by Philip Hardwick, and its pairs of lodges. It symbolised the first trunk railway of the world which united London and Birmingham. How much more imaginative is this subtle use of an open space. 'The thickness and fullness are, currently, components of the viability of space in the context of architectural problems with which the future is confronted', as one of our foremost architectural critics so ably put it. These two monoliths are of unequal height, so as to show the un-regimentation of modern architecture. They are the Doric columns of today. What do they represent? Surely everyone knows that we don't want representational art. We want art to stand on its own merits, like abstract sculpture. Well, these are the abstract sculptures of British Rail. Maybe one of them tries to let out the diesel fumes from the taxi rank, and the other is something to do with the air-conditioning in the Main Circulating Area. I don't think it matters, do you? And if you do happen to like representational art, then Stephenson, who designed the railway, has his statue which used to stand in the Great Hall. But I think that forward looking readers won't want such monuments.

London Railway Stations

FLOWER OF CITIES: A BOOK OF LONDON. 1949

The study of railway stations is something like the study of churches. It can be turned into archaeological detection work. For piscina, read cast-iron lamp bracket; for arcading, read girder construction; for transepts, read waiting-rooms; for hangings, read tin advertisements. Then with very little practice anyone with an eye for detail can date the objects inspected.

Picture a disused platform of a rather forgotten station, let us say South Hampstead, the first station after Euston (2½ miles) on the old L.M.S. electric line to Watford. It opens late and shuts early and few people seem to use it. When I was a boy we called it Loudon Road and the booking office building stood, as it still stands, looking rather like a small mid-Victorian brick Vicarage, harmonising happily with the Gothic fancies of this lilac-shaded part of St John's Wood. I should think from the style of architecture it was built in the late seventies by which time enough platforms had been constructed at Euston to make it possible for the London & North Western to run an enlarged suburban service. I have never departed from nor alighted at South Hampstead. Not being modern, my hours are too long either side of the day to take advantage of its times of opening. I prefer to imagine the station. I like to think that it contains the various fittings of a former age for which my eye is always on the watch when I use an unfamiliar station. Perhaps there are some very old tickets in the booking office – a first-class return to Chalk Farm (which would

[103]

mean going down to Euston and coming back again), would probably be printed with 'Loudon Road' and the letters L.N.W.R. Under the treads of the stairs to the platform there may be those tin advertisements saying IRON JELLOIDS, IRON JELLOIDS, IRON JELLOIDS in blue on an orange ground, insisting, as one ascends, on the weakness of one's heart and its need for the stamina which those pills supply. Still in imagination, I walk right down to the end of the platform to the oldest lamp standard, a graceful thing on twisted columns with, perhaps, a six-sided glass cage for the gas-burner and the name of the iron foundry where it was made at the base of its column. Against the station wall there may be tin signs for MAZAWATTEE TEA and the still-familiar black and blue splodge of STEPHEN'S INK on a white ground. And, of course, there will be those two old friends VENO'S LIGHTNING COUGH CURE and DR. J. COLLIS BROWNE'S CHLORODYNE.

Then what waiting rooms may there not be! Gothic Revival cast-iron grates in which no fire has been lighted since the days when a mountain of glowing coal warmed the early-morning pin-striped bottoms of city gentlemen who used this station as the preliminary part of a journey from Boundary Road to Euston, thence by steam train on the inner circle from Euston Square to Aldersgate. The walls of the waiting room will be green. The lighting gas. There will perhaps be a framed collection of photographs, 'Beauty Spots' of the L. & N.W.R. – Killarney; Sackville Street, Dublin; Blarney Castle (the L. & N.W. always liked to give the impression that it owned all the Irish railways); George's Landing Stage, Liverpool; Bettws-y-coed; Warwick Castle. These will be in sepia with gilt lettering on the wooden surround. Then there will be a framed looking-glass in which it will be impossible to see all one's face because painted on the surface are the words IDRIS TABLE WATERS and a long maiden in clothes rather like a water lily holding in her hand a sparkling glass of IDRIS. These are but some of the delights I imagine there may be at South Hampstead.

The serious scholar of London railway stations will make the historical approach. I unfold the map of my *Bradshaw's Railway Companion for 1841*. London shrinks to its size a hundred and nine years ago. I notice that there were fields beyond Regent's Park and Pentonville and Islington and Hackney. Bethnal Green was in London, Stratford was not. Southeast of Bermondsey and south of Walworth there were still fields between terraces and squares, fields that in two years were to be filled with either Italianate merchants' houses amid laurel shrubbery or with rows of two-storey artisans' dwellings. Chelsea and Brompton and Kensington still had separate personalities. No railways dared to invade the centre of London. Westminster was even more sacred than the City. There they are on the map, little pink lines, pushing tentatively towards the heart of the metropolis.

These early stations, you must remember, are part of the Georgian age. They are stately but not sumptuous. They are spreading but not soaring. They suggest coaches pulled by iron horses. They are merely another sort of posting inn, not something private, railed off and of another world, which railways have now become. They are the stables of the iron horses and they blend naturally with the drays which clatter over cobbles towards them and the carriages which are unloaded from them and pulled away by horses to the noblemen's houses of Mayfair. Euston (1837), London Bridge (1838), Paddington (1839) are still on their original sites. Philip Hardwick's magnificent Doric Arch of granite (1837) at Euston originally had two lodges flanking each side and was visible from the Euston Road; the outer pairs of these have been destroyed. It was the gateway not only to all the country houses of the North, but also to a new age. The little iron sheds of the station behind it, so ridiculed by Pugin, are rather an anti-climax. Successive generations have treated this noble arch scurvily and its glory has been hidden by the Euston Hotel. As an essay of the Greek Revival, I consider the arch even now, almost shorn of its lodges, the noblest thing in London, nobler even than St Pancras Church or the British Museum or the Hyde Park Screen. Only one building rivalled it and that was Rennie's Waterloo Bridge. The L.M.S. made determined efforts to remove Euston Arch altogether. British Railways will probably succeed in doing so, for no one, except you and me, dear reader, yet believes that there can be anything beautiful about a railway station.

London Bridge, now a shattered collection of girders and temporary-looking platforms, has little to show of the old terminus of the Greenwich Railway, that remarkable line carried on 878 brick arches, which was merged with the South-Eastern and Chatham. There is a spacious dignity, created by white brick walls and an arching roof, about the Terminus part of the station whence trains depart over a loop line via the Crystal Palace (Low Level) and Norwood to Victoria, through Italianate stations and brick cuttings and sudden elevations from which one may see the brick Italianate houses of Ruskin's South London, the prehistoric monsters of the Crystal Palace Park and perhaps glimpse Sherlock Holmes hiding amid the laurels, lamp posts and ivy-clad clinker of a merchant's private drive.

The severe nine-arched entrance of Paddington has disappeared entirely, though the space in front of where it stood, now under glass, is still known as 'the lawn'. But two others of these six early stations survive. Nine Elms, erected in 1838 by Sir William Tite (architect of the Royal Exchange) as the terminus of the South Western Railway, may be found standing, classic, stuccoed and deserted, amid the gasworks, goods yards and factories of that district where strikes seem often to originate. There are no passengers and the more important goods yards seem to be in another part of Nine Elms, so that this building and its platforms are an early station survival.* I know of no more complete example except Philip Hardwick's Great Arch at the old and disused terminus in Birmingham of the London to Birmingham Railway.

A smaller London station of this period is now out of reach of the public. It is the Blackwall terminus of the old London and Blackwall Railway. Those frequent and quite empty trains of the Blackwall Railway ran from a special platform of Fenchurch Street. I remember them well. Like stage-coaches they rumbled slowly past East-End chimney pots, wharves and shipping, stopping at black and empty stations, till they came to a final halt at Blackwall station, a handsome building in white brick and Portland stone, from an Italianate design by Sir William Tite. When one emerged there was nothing to see beyond it but a cobbled quay and a vast stretch of wind-whipped water, over one of the broadest tidal reaches of the Thames.

There may be, among the bomb damage, some remains of Bricklayers' Arms Station (1840), long demoted, like Nine Elms, to a goods depot. Bricklayers' Arms was known as the 'West End Terminus' of the South Eastern Railway and marks probably the first and last time the Old Kent Road has been described as the West End of London. It was a classic structure.†

Somewhere, too, among the arches, goods yards and stables down a side street off Shoreditch one may be still be able to find remains of the old Terminus of the Eastern Union Railway (1839) which was designed by Sancton Wood. It was the precursor of Liverpool Street and its architect was a pupil of Sir Robert Smirke and like his master a bold classicist. He designed the palatial Roman terminus of Kingsbridge, Dublin (1845), with its twin cupolas, and Leinster Square, Paddington, and part of Hyde Park Gardens.

By the fifties, the old coaching view of railways was out of date. They were establishing an architecture of their own and as keenly as Tractarians and Evangelicals they joined in the Battle of the Styles, Classic v. Gothic. On the whole the Classic style won. Euston, long a pioneer in railway architecture, set the tone with the Euston Great Hall which was completed in 1849. It was the joint design of old Philip Hardwick and his son Philip Charles Hardwick. Never had there been and never has there been since in England so magnificent a piece of railway architecture. This huge hall is now ruined with filthy little kiosks and enquiry bureaux built in a jazz-modern style by the L.M.S. But not even these destroy its proportions and it is still possible to note its double staircase, its rich ceiling, its figured

*Now the new Covent Garden fruit, vegetable and flower market.
† Cubitt's frontage was damaged by fire in 1936 and demolished. The station has been derelict for the last ten years and British Rail are in the process of selling the site for housing development.

consols supporting the ceiling and carved by John Thomas, who made the figures and bosses in the Houses of Parliament. At the top of the staircase, and not open to the public, is the room for the Shareholders' General Meetings, an untouched specimen of Roman Revival of the late forties. This sumptuous hall and offices set the fashion for railway architecture. Even the chairs of waiting rooms and desks in the offices had a Roman grandeur about them, executed in oak and mahogany, solid and heavy as a Christmas dinner. To compare with Euston, there is nothing. Other lines as they built their termini and chief suburban stations went in for classic, but the classic style preferred was that of the French Renaissance. It may be seen in those stations of the sixties, Charing Cross, Cannon Street, Broad Street, Farringdon Street, Aldersgate, Highbury, Bow, Camden Town, and it even survived into the next decade when Holborn Viaduct Station was built.

The architect of Charing Cross and Cannon Street was Edward Middleton Barry, a son of Sir Charles, the architect of the Houses of Parliament. Edward's masterpiece is undoubtedly the Charing Cross Hotel (1864). I know few pleasanter meeting places than the first floor of that building. A broad staircase leads to corridors done in the manner of Sir John Soane, unexpectedly Graeco-Roman when there is so much French Renaissance about the exterior. On this floor is the suite of rooms I call 'the club'. There is a smoking room with bar attached and billiard room adjoining and one can walk on to a balcony, drink in hand, to survey the crowds and trains of the station below. There are horse-hair seats in the smoking

St Pancras Station

room, a bookshelf with a set of Shakespeare and a guide to the Southern Railway, and one has the place to oneself, while all around in stately dining rooms, private luncheons are being held by old-fashioned boards of directors, the Ouse Catchment Board, the Blackwall Tunnel Company, the Tower Hamlets Development Society, the United Kingdom Union of Persecuting Protestants. Much of this activity used to occur at the Cannon Street Hotel (1866) designed by the same architect. The station itself at Cannon Street is a far finer building that that at Charing Cross which has been deprived of its original semi-circular roof. Barry's towers and cupolas at the river opening of Cannon Street compare well with Wren's steeples and blend this great structure into the steepled outline of the City.

The only time the Great Western went in for Classic in a big way was when it employed Philip Charles Hardwick to design the Paddington Hotel in the sixties. The dining room here with its curving caryatids, probably by John Thomas, was almost up to the standard of Euston's Graeco-Roman office buildings. Just before the Hitler war this dining room, or 'Coffee Room' as it was called, was ruined by being streamlined with plywood in a jazz-modern manner, so that it is now like any semi-smart new restaurant. The Great Western otherwise has been fairly loyal to Tudor, a style which it first adopted at Temple Meads, Bristol, and still employs there. The only nearly untouched examples of a Tudor station on the London to Bristol line which survive are Shrivenham and Box. There was an unfortunate period in the nineteen-thirties when the Great Western went 'Modern' in the Great West Road sense of that word, with its new office buildings at Paddington. It adopted at this time too that hideous monogram on its engines. When Paddington Station was rebuilt the company employed Digby Wyatt on architectural effects.

The richest Gothic station is, of course, St Pancras (1868). The enormous iron and glass roof with a clear span of 240 feet, 100 feet high and 700 feet long, makes the trains and platforms below it look like a model railway. It was designed by P. W. Barlow, the Civil Engineer. The tie beams that hold it are below the station and form a roof for the enormous vaults, which are under the whole area of the station. The hotel which is attached to the station, but not related to it, is by Sir Gilbert Scott. Ferguson much objected to it. 'There is no proportion between the shed and its uses, and everything looks out of place, and most of all the Gothic mouldings and brick work, borrowed from the domestic architecture of the Middle Ages, which thrusts itself beween the gigantic iron ribs of the roof.'

Ferguson did not like the Gothic Revival, and even Sir Gilbert does not seem to have been wholly enthusiastic about St Pancras Hotel. Never one to underestimate his own work, he says of it: 'My own belief is that it is possibly *too good* for its purpose, but having been disappointed, through Lord Palmerston, of my ardent hope of carrying out my style in the

Government offices, and the subject having been in the meanwhile taken out of my hands by other architects, I was glad to be able to erect one building in that style in London.'

The hotel is now, alas, offices. But the splendid intertwining double staircase of ironwork survives (in the well of this there used to be a Turkish kiosk for coffee) and the huge Arthurian style wallpapers are to be found here and there. The refreshment rooms have all been jazzed, and only the station booking hall remains as an untouched Scott interior.* Alongside

St Pancras is the Midland goods station whose brickwork is undoubtedly the best in London. Sir Gilbert, like his grandson Sir Giles, was always interested in brick and stonework and for the goods station he had bricks specially made of varying sizes. You may see in the screen wall of the building (with its exquisite iron grilles) that the bricks grow smaller as they go higher, giving an effect of solidity to the wall.

Of the exterior of the hotel I am myself enamoured. The clock tower has always seemed to me a highly picturesque outline and the rows of middle-pointed windows along the whole curving sweep achieve an effect of unity with diversity. As a practical plan for an hotel, the building is appalling. But as an exercise in scale and the skilful use of brick and stone it is unsurpassed in railway architecture. All other Midland stations in London are an anti-climax, as though the company had ruined itself on St Pancras and had to be content with mere wooden sheds and brick booking

*A project to rehabilitate the chambers and turn them back into an hotel and the present booking hall into a banqueting hall is being developed by a major property company.

halls for the rest of the system. Fenchurch Street, which it took over from the London, Tilbury and Southend Railway, is a humbler affair more in the manner of (and but a few years later than) the Great Northern Railway terminus of King's Cross.

This building, which Ferguson describes as the more successful and pleasing 'plainer sister' of St Pancras, is entirely the work of the engineer Joseph Cubitt. It was built in 1851 and the materials are white brick, glass and iron. The purpose at once is plain. One great semi-circular archway is for departure, the other beside it is for arrival. Between them on the main front is appropriately placed a clock tower. A colonnade of brick arches runs along the base of this front, between vast brick buttresses, and acts as a shelter for those awaiting their carriages. The booking office is on the departure side of the building and opposite this is a crescent-shaped hotel in a simple white-brick and stone, classic style. Office buildings balance this on the arrival side of the station. The coherence of the design is now much hampered by an underground station and by shops which hide its truthful simplicity from the Euston Road. Ruskin said in the *Seven Lamps of Architecture*, 'Better bury gold in the embankments than put it in ornaments on the stations . . . Railroad architecture has, or would have, a dignity of its own, if it were only left to its work. You would not put rings on the fingers of a smith at his anvil.' He must surely have approved of King's Cross, though he makes no specific mention of it. It is certainly the only London station which is pure railway architecture. I have always thought the new Underground stations (except that at Hammersmith) self-consciously simple in comparison with King's Cross. They are so much aware that they are in the 'modern style', so tastefully arranged with red brick on the street level, and so streamlined that they smack more of the advertising agency than the railway.

King's Cross started no new style, except at different stations on its own line beyond London. The nearest approach to it, other than Fenchurch Street, is Liverpool Street which was built in the seventies. It is civil engineer's Gothic, rather than architect's Gothic, and none the worse for that. The Gothic-style iron pillars support many-vistaed arcading, the flattened arch of the roof is crenellated on its own hanging edge and many mouldings and capitals in ironwork are to be found by the careful observer. Indeed, on a foggy evening, when those pear-shaped arc lamps used to hang down low from the roof, casting a purplish-white light, Liverpool Street had quite a resemblance to an ancient abbey.

The last large station to be built in London was Marylebone (1899) for the Great Central Railway. Its buildings are of hard pink midland bricks with yellow terra-cotta dressings and all in Flemish Renaissance style. They look like a public library from Nottingham which has unexpectedly found itself in London. A beautiful description of this station and of the Great Central Railway is to be found in Mr Hamilton Ellis's *The Trains*

We Loved. The weakness of the Great Central for gorgeous decorations in its carriages did not extend to stations; but its luxury is commemorated in Colonel Edis's gorgeous Great Central Hotel on the Marylebone Road. This entirely dwarfs the quiet terminus behind it.

There is no doubt that Marylebone set a new tone to London Railway architecture. Henceforward something more tasteful than the flimsy wooden constructions was considered suitable for suburban stations. The L. & N.W.R. employed the noted domestic architect Gerald Horsley in 1901 to design stations at Harrow and Pinner in a style half-way between that of a bank and a medium-sized country house. Harrow, with its tower, was remarkably successful. Termini were thought to be ornate in the wrong sort of way, too like the Louvre and not enough like Michael Angelo. So there were the great rebuildings in an Edwardian monumental Renaissance manner starting with the L.B. & S.C. in 1908 at Victoria. The most ponderous effort of all was Waterloo with its twenty-three platforms and vast, useless entrance arch, approached by flights of steps unlike Euston, symbolical of nothing. Baker Street by Charles W. Clarke was a quieter building for the Metropolitan Railway in the neo-Georgian style (1914). Its refreshment rooms are still untouched. The most charming of all the Edwardian and neo-Georgian Renaissance stations is the entrance to Charing Cross Underground by H. W. Ford (1913). Marble columns in restaurants, stained glass, thick and crinkly, and adorned with wreaths, Turkey carpets, bronze or beaten copper electroliers, mahogany

screens with panels of bevelled glass, plaster-work in the baroque manner, external sculpture in the manner of Sir Hamo Thorneycroft as at Waterloo – all these are characteristic of the last age of Railway Architecture. Redecorations in this manner went on in nearly every station. The hotel at Liverpool Street sustained such refittings and even at the St Pancras Hotel a dining room was redecorated in a 'Georgian' style.

Such is the stylistic development of the London railways until the dismal grouping and the even more dismal eclipse of all individuality which has now occurred. But just as in a church architecture is not so important as the worship which goes on there, so in railways the associations of a station and of a line are part of its beauty. The personality of most stations in London survives, even through British Railways, and will continue to do so until everyone in England is exactly the same as everyone else.

Waterloo is the 'services' and race-goers' station – for 'Pompey', 'Soton', Aldershot, Epsom, Ascot. It has a rather high-class suburban connection. Civil Servants who have reached CMG and knighthood stage will find it near Whitehall and convenient for Esher and in pine-clad Southern Electric suburbs their wives play cards with wives of rich city gentlemen. The humbler Civil Servant uses the Metropolitan and moves outwards beyond to Rickmansworth and Northwood as his salary increases. He probably knows he is not going to reach the heights of Esher Civil Servants and there is no point in establishing a railway carriage connection on the Southern Electric. The commercial people who use the Metropolitan are in their turn slightly less rich than the city gentlemen who use Waterloo.

The flashiest of all suburban travellers are those who travel daily from Victoria by first-class Pullman trains to Brighton. Indeed, Brighton so dominates Victoria Station that though continental trains depart from its South Eastern Section, though many of the inner London suburbs are served by puzzling loop lines which start here and end at London Bridge, Victoria is the station of what moneyed leisure is left in London. Though it is meant to be associated with the South Coast and summer holidays, the sea is not what one associates with those who use it regularly. They do not look as though they took a winter dip in the English Channel. Warm flats, television, cocktail cabinets and bridge seem to be more in their line.

What a contrast is Liverpool Street! Here those extraordinary, cramped and uncomfortable Great Eastern carriages are drawn out above the East End housetops to wide acres of Essex suburb, two-storey houses, flat recreation grounds, strange chapels of strange sects, the well-trodden commons on the fringes of Epping Forest. Here workmen's trains run early in the morning. Here the old London sulphur smell pervades and even red bricks receive a black coating. Dense streets of Tottenham, Wanstead, Leytonstone, Barking, Edmonton, you are the real London and you form a barrier between the town and the unspoiled country of East Anglia! So many trains carry your patient passengers in and out of the black cathedral of Liverpool Street that expresses to Harwich, Yarmouth and Norwich seem slow at starting and ending for fear, no doubt, of knocking into one of these hundreds of suburban steam trains. Fenchurch Street has the same quality as Liverpool Street and so has London Bridge.

Charing Cross is the railway's concession to the Continent. Though it is possible to leave Charing Cross for Kent, the impression travellers like to give when they use Charing Cross is that they are going abroad. Little Bureaux de Change at the entrance encourage the impression and Edward Middleton Barry's elaborate Eleanor Cross, befouled by pigeons in the station yard, reminds us once more of one of Europe's shining gifts to England, Eleanor of Castile.

I do not know what to say of Cannon Street. Of all the stations of London it is my favourite, so echoing, so lofty and so sad. Whoever used it and who uses it now? Holborn Viaduct was the great station for hop-pickers on their journey to Kent. But Cannon Street is too stately for that sort of thing. It is much less important than London Bridge at which most of its trains stop. Perhaps the people of Bromley, that lonely high-class suburb in Kent, love Cannon Street as I do.

There is one station, however, which hardly anyone uses at all – Broad Street,* which is given over to ghosts of frock-coated citizens who once crowded the old North London trains from the steam suburbs of Highbury, Canonbury and Camden Town. Often do those sumptuous L.M.S. electric trains swing across the North London suburbs on that smooth, useless, beautiful journey to Richmond. At no time of day have I known it impossible to find a seat in their spacious carriages. And the frock-coated ones are dead and gone like the rolling stock which carried them, their houses have been turned into flats, their gardens built over by factories. The North London was the last line to use wooden-seated third-class carriages as it did on its Poplar branch (now closed), the last line in London to run no trains during church time on a Sunday morning, and within living memory the General Manager of the line refused to allow Smith's bookstall on Broad Street to sell any vulgar-looking papers. Still the trains run, through haunted gas-lit stations, on the most revealing railway journey London can provide.

The main line platforms of King's Cross are all expresses and Civil Servants bagging the first-class sleepers to Scotland, their fares paid for them out of our taxes. I do not like it, despite its noble architecture. It is a station, like Euston, that those few of us who are not Civil Servants will associate with injustice. But these dim suburban platforms at King's Cross

*Demolished 1985. An office development called Broadgate is being built on the site.

to which trains come puffing up from the inner circle, are still Victorian London. Here runs much uncomfortable rolling stock to Barnet and Hatfield, climbing slowly to Finsbury Park. All the money is spent on streamling those L.N.E.R. expresses in the main station.

St Pancras is a station apart, a Royal Station. The old idea that the Midland was the most comfortable railway in the world still holds good despite the strenuous efforts of the L.M.S. to kill it. There is a suburban service, but it is of no importance. I have the impression that St Pancras is still the aristocratic route to Scotland. Gun-cases and fishing-rods go north with tweed-clad lairds, salmon and game returning in the guard's van without them. I have little doubt that British Railways will do away with St Pancras altogether. It is too beautiful and too romantic to survive. It is not of this age. Euston has stolen its trains but not its atmosphere. Except for that concealed platform where the Irish mail leaves of an evening, there is no personality left about the trains from Euston. To the Irish, Euston is the chief of English stations. Even lesser stations on the line are written on their minds for I know of an Irish Peer who woke up during a Wagner Opera at Covent Garden and exclaimed: 'Just like Willesden Junction!'

Except for Broad Street, Marylebone is the quietest station. Only two expresses leave it in a day, the 'South Yorkshireman' and the 'Master Cutler'. There is hardly room for more and the suburban service to Buckinghamshire seems like an after-thought. I have never met anyone who has used one of the Marylebone expresses, but lately I had the pleasure of coming into Marylebone on a semi-express which stopped at Brackley. We rushed through late Victorian cuttings and under bridges of glazed brick, nearly merging with the Metropolitan. When I reached London I found I was one of fifteen passengers.

Paddington has the strongest personality of all the larger London stations. Its passengers are nearly all country people. There is the one exception, a large contingent of South Welsh who seem always to be travelling in trains. There is a lessening section of old-fashioned people, too poor now to travel first, who come up on the cheap day fares from Wiltshire and Gloucestershire to visit the Army and Navy Stores. Relations from further west stay a night or two at the Paddington Hotel. There are some Oxford dons and at holiday times more schoolboys than on any other line. Add to them a final section of commuters who have transformed Newbury and Maidenhead, Reading and Henley into suburbs of London.

I am aware that this attempt at the atmosphere of London stations is sketchy. Sketchy and no doubt unfair, for there must be many to whom King's Cross and Euston are charming places and others who detest Cannon Street, St Pancras and Liverpool Street as I do not. To them I apologise, but if I have caused them to think of these stations as places with the strong personalities that only those who use them can know, I will have achieved my object. To me they are people, and people have sides to their characters that they reveal to some and not to others.

Coffee, Port and Cigars
on the Inner Circle

THE TIMES. 24 MAY 1963

Each line on the Underground system had a distinct personality. From about 1916 until 1921 I used the holidays for travelling over the system, so that there was not a station at which I had not alighted. The result is that the Underground map of London is firmly imprinted in my mind and from Golders Green to Clapham Common, from New Cross to Ealing Broadway, from Finsbury Park to Hammersmith, I know the stations by heart.

I remember Park Royal as a little wooden platform, high above the football ground of the Queen's Park Rangers and what a pleasant walk one could take by leafy lanes and elmy fields of Middlesex between Preston Road Station on the Metropolitan to the newly electrified Kenton Station on the extension beyond Queen's Park of the Bakerloo. It is surprising how little the map has changed and even the colours used to denote the different lines have in many cases continued until the present day. During the First World War these colours were: red for the Metropolitan, green for the District, grey for the City and South London, blue for the Central London, orange for the Great Northern and City and brown, yellow and violet for the Bakerloo, Piccadilly and Hampstead lines respectively of the London Electric Railway Company.

Electricity was in the air and gas was on the way out. Electricity stood for cleanliness, quietness, hygiene, swiftness and progress. By electricity the City clerk could glide, when he had left the Underground at the bottom of Highgate Hill at a station euphemistically called Highgate, by electric tram to North Finchley and from Edgware Road he could take another electric tram to Harlesden, while at Shepherd's Bush and Hammersmith there was a choice of tramway routes out into the flat hay fields and market gardens which still held out in West Middlesex against the oncoming villas.

The line with the dominating personality in the system was the Metropolitan. Since it had started in the age of steam, as the first Underground and had a nasty reputation for sulphur and soot, it was most anxious to live down its past. The Inner Circle, which it shared with the District Railway, was electrified and so was its line from Baker Street to Swiss Cottage and beyond. Only the smoke-blackened, brown bricks of its stations in the tunnels and the shapely round glass globes enclosing gaslights illuminating such stations as Bayswater, Praed Street, Notting Hill Gate,

Portland Road and Euston Square, Marlborough Road and Swiss Cottage, reminded one that this line had once been steam. Under that great general manager Mr R. H. Selbie, the Metropolitan invented Metroland and the phrase 'Beechy Bucks' and by means of enticing sepia photographs in its carriages, brochures and refreshment rooms – 'Cottage at Prestwood', 'Near Great Missenden', 'Haydon Hall, Eastcote', 'At Ickenham' – tempted the Londoner out on to new estates, far beyond the Wembley Exhibition. The line affected a white-tiled classical style just after the First World War, as may be seen still at Farringdon Street, and below the Portland stone cliffs of Chiltern Court and at Edgware Road it tried to forget the steamy origins of huge echoing, iron-roofed stations like Aldersgate Street where, until the Second World War, there used to be a notice in white china letters on the windows of the refreshment room 'Afternoon Teas a Speciality'. The Metropolitan stretched its tentacles round the Inner Circle to Mansion House and South Kensington, over the Great Western to Hammersmith, eastward to Whitechapel and it even had running powers over the London and South Western to Richmond. There was an inexplicable branch to Addison Road, while the District, never a line with so much personality, ran its red carriages up to Uxbridge Road and west to the Ealings and Actons and Uxbridge. The poor relation of these lines, was the East London, from Shoreditch, with two stations at New Cross and green diamonds behind the names of the stations and very few advertisements on the platforms, because the people who used the line were so poor that they were not considered worth advertisements.

There was one mysterious line, which differed from the rest in having larger tunnels and rolling stock, and this was the Great Northern and City, from Finsbury Park to Moorgate, which had been opened in 1904. The line still seems to be out on a limb and Drayton Park has always seemed to me the remotest of the older Underground stations, just as Essex Road is the least used, now that City Road, South Kentish Town, York Road, Brompton Road and Down Street have been shut.

The City and South London was the first real 'tube' electric railway, and it still had, when I first knew it, the atmosphere of 1890, the year of its opening. Little orange engines carried rolling stock, with basket seats and cut glass electric lights. Many of the platforms, as still to be seen at Angel, King's Cross and south of the river, were central and narrow, with trains running either side of them so that there was a temptation to fling oneself on to the live line. The whole railway had a strong smell of wet feet or a changing room after games and the line was delightfully uneven, so that one could look down the length of the carriages and see them switchbacking up and down, behind or before one. The Waterloo and City, which belonged to the London and South Western, never really counted in my mind as part of the system any more than 'the elevated electric' from Victoria to London Bridge. But the Waterloo and City was allowed to

appear on the Underground maps and it had a smell, engines and rolling stock slightly similar to the City and South London.

The Central London from Bank to Wood Lane, extended to Liverpool Street in 1912, was the highest class line because it went by Bond Street to the City. It was also regarded as a sort of health resort, because it was ventilated by the Ozonair system, which was meant to smell like the sea, and certainly did smell of something. Air came out of grilles at the ends of huge aluminium pipes and sent a health-giving breeze down the platforms which caused the crinkly glass shades which hung over the white tiled stations to move slightly. The carriages had basket seats and were, as on all Underground lines, operated by men who pulled open the gates between the carriages at the stations. The Central London went in for terra cotta above ground and one may still see the outside of the old British Museum station where High Holborn and New Oxford Street join.

The Bakerloo was one of the enterprises of the share pusher and art connoisseur, Whitaker Wright, but he died in 1904 and the line was not opened until 1906. I have often thought that his artistic taste may however have pervaded the three railways of the London Electric Railway Company – the Bakerloo, the Piccadilly and Brompton, the Hampstead and Highgate. All these lines had, and still have, stations above ground of red shiny tiles in a classical style. The doors of the lifts had an *art nouveau* pierced pattern in their ironwork and the stations below were built with bands of different coloured tiles; for instance, Covent Garden, orange; Dover Street (now Green Park) dove grey; Goodge Street, green; York road, yellow; so that the traveller, who came to a halt not opposite the station name, could tell where he was by the colour. The colours seem to have been chosen on some principle of alliteration and association. These stations do not seem to have been designed originally for advertisements, for here and there along the tiles were little *art nouveau* notice spaces, made of tiles, presumably for timetables and rules and regulations.

The chief difference between the London Underground of today and that of 1918 is in the number of passengers. Far fewer people travelled by Underground. Not only was London much smaller and the system less extensive, but people preferred travelling on the open tops of buses and the half protected tops of trams. They could see the streets and buildings, for road traffic was less congested. Down below the earth, as one sat on those basket seats, there used to be a silence like deep country after the man between the carriages had opened the trellis work gates and footsteps of the few passengers could be heard walking towards draughty passage and shuddering lift. Lancaster Gate Station still has some of this atmosphere.

The District Railway, in an effort to eclipse the Metropolitan, was ahead of its time when it made that desperate liaison with the London Tilbury and Southend. For a time it ran express trains, stopping at most stations, from Ealing Broadway to Southend and I can recall Pullman carriages passing through Sloane Square Station. Now that the main roads of London are so much less attractive than the tunnels underneath, ventures such as these might well be revived. I have long wished to travel round the Inner Circle in a dining car – hors d'oeuvres at South Kensington, fish at the Monument, joint at Baker Street, cheese at Notting Hill Gate, and perhaps once round again with the coffee, port and cigars.

The Metropolitan Railway
Baker Street Station Buffet

Early Electric! With what radiant hope
  Men formed this many-branched electrolier,
Twisted the flex around the iron rope
  And let the dazzling vacuum globes hang clear,
And then with hearts the rich contrivance fill'd
Of copper, beaten by the Bromsgrove Guild.

Early Electric! Sit you down and see
  'Mid this fine woodwork and a smell of dinner,
A stained-glass windmill and a pot of tea,
  The sepia views of leafy lanes in PINNER,
Then visualize, far down the shining lines,
Your parents' homestead set in murmuring pines.

Smoothly from HARROW, passing PRESTON ROAD,
  They saw the last green fields and misty sky,
At NEASDEN watch'd a workman's train unload
  And, with the morning villas sliding by,
They felt so sure on their electric trip
That Youth and Progress were in partnership.

And all that day in murky London Wall
  The thought of RUISLIP kept him warm inside;
At FARRINGDON that lunch hour at a stall
  He bought a dozen plants of London Pride;
While she, in arc-lit Oxford Street adrift,
Soared through the sales by safe hydraulic lift.

Early Electric! Maybe even here
  They met that evening at six-fifteen
Beneath the hearts of this electrolier
  And caught the first non-stop to WILLESDEN GREEN,
Then out and on, through rural RAYNER'S LANE
To autumn-scented Middlesex again.

Cancer has killed him. Heart is killing her.
  The trees are down. An Odeon flashes fire
Where stood their villa by the murmuring fir
  When "they would for their children's good conspire."
Of all their loves and hopes on hurrying feet
Thou art the worn memorial, Baker Street.

[121]

CHURCHES

Outside St Mary-le-Strand

The Grosvenor Chapel

Introduction to Ann Callender (Ed.) GODLY MAYFAIR. 1980

I have always liked things which hide themselves. This the Grosvenor Chapel certainly does. From the outside you would never know what a surprise awaited you architecturally. Outside it is a little piece of New England in warm old London brick set down amid fashionable Dutch revival commercial premises of the eighties onwards.

It is the Chapel's quietness and obscurity which have made me fond of it, and the fact that it is High Church, which I was brought up and am. I first went there because it was a continuation of the Oxford I had known and loved as an undergraduate in the twenties, and I have always liked its associations with Oxford. It was run in those days by Philip Usher, an unassuming, quiet and scholarly priest like Wilfred Derry who later followed him. I went because of Freddie Hood. He was such a good man. You could see when he looked out at you through his wire spectacles that he knew everything about you: his eyes twinkled with understanding and affection.

On the whole, what makes Grosvenor Chapel perfect for me is that people never bother you there. The whole point of it is that you aren't asked to join something. The joy of going there is that you aren't being welcomed into a club and made to go to parties and take part in things. You are left alone, but at the same time you aren't cold shouldered.

I remember getting to know the Chapel better in Father Whiteman's day, because Rose Macaulay was a good friend of mine, and she loved Father Whiteman. Once, when the ice was very cold and thick on the Serpentine, it was said Rose petitioned Father Whiteman to break it so that she could bathe. When dear old Joad was dying of cancer, Father Whiteman used to bring the sacrament out from Grosvenor Chapel to Hampstead and Rose and I used to attend mass there in his house with Father Whiteman as the celebrant.

Another reason why I belong to Grosvenor Chapel is that its depth and beauty have grown on me. I do not think that it is even necessary to complete Comper's uncompleted scheme. The building has got a little bit of mystery to it in its unfinished state. Comper had an absolutely unerring sense of where to put things. Grosvenor Chapel is a real church with mystery in it. It is a real adornment to Mayfair. It is in the natural material of London, which is brick. It partakes of the Thames Valley, although its interior is by an Aberdonian Scot. And it has got a surprising greatness of scale, which you would not guess from the outside. It is also extremely comfortable: it is upholstered religion for the rich.

The preaching tradition is fine. The best preacher I know is John Gaskell. I am very glad to say that I am a sermon taster, and I have never heard better sermons than his. He has the natural melody of language in his words. He is obviously a poet. In fact, Grosvenor Chapel is a most surprising church in that it is such a poetical place. We don't want argument. We want to be carried away into the heavens, as we are there. And when we step out and we see Purdey's, it's very surprising – everything is a surprising contrast.

opposite: a school by E. R. Robson

South London Sketch, 1944

From Bermondsey to Wandsworth
  So many churches are,
Some with apsidal chancels,
  Some Perpendicular
And schools by E. R. Robson
  In the style of Norman Shaw
Where blue-serged adolescence learn'd
  To model and to draw.

Oh, in among the houses,
  The viaduct below,
Stood the Coffee Essence Factory
  Of Robinson and Co.
Burnt and brown and tumbled down
  And done with years ago
Where the waters of the Wandle do
  Lugubriously flow.

From dust of dead explosions,
  From scarlet-hearted fires,
All unconcerned this train draws in
  And smoothly that retires
And calmly rise on smoky skies
  Of intersected wires
The Nonconformist spirelets
  And the Church of England spires.

[125]

St. Saviour's, Aberdeen Park, Highbury, London, N.*

With oh such peculiar branching and over-reaching of wire
Trolley-bus standards pick their threads from the London sky.
Diminishing up the perspective, Highbury-bound retire
Threads and buses and standards with plane trees volleying by
And, more peculiar still, that ever-increasing spire
Bulges over the housetops, polychromatic and high.

Stop the trolley-bus, stop! And here, where the roads unite
    Of weariest worn-out London – no cigarettes, no beer,
No repairs undertaken, nothing in stock – alight;
    For over the waste of willow-herb, look at her, sailing clear,
A great Victorian church, tall, unbroken and bright
    In a sun that's setting in Willesden and saturating us here.

These were the streets my parents knew when they loved and won –
The brougham that crunched the gravel, the laurel-girt paths that wind,
Geranium-beds for the lawn, Venetian blinds for the sun,
A separate tradesman's entrance, straw in the mews behind,
Just in the four-mile radius where hackney carriages run,
    Solid Italianate houses for the solid commercial mind.

These were the streets they knew; and I, by descent, belong
    To these tall neglected houses divided into flats.
Only the church remains, where carriages used to throng
And my mother stepped out in flounces and my father stepped out
in spats
To shadowy stained-glass matins or gas-lit evensong
    And back in a country quiet with doffing of chimney hats.

Great red church of my parents, cruciform crossing they knew –
    Over these same encaustics they and their parents trod
Bound through a red-brick transept for a once familiar pew
Where the organ set them singing and the sermon let them nod
And up this coloured brickwork the same long shadows grew
As these in the stencilled chancel where I kneel in the presence of God.

*Restored by English Heritage in 1986.

Wonder beyond Time's wonders, that Bread so white and small
  Veiled in golden curtains, too mighty for men to see,
Is the Power which sends the shadows up this polychrome wall,
  Is God who created the present, the chain-smoking millions and me;
Beyond the throb of the engines is the throbbing heart of all –
  Christ, at this Highbury altar, I offer myself To Thee.

Westminster Abbey

Prologue to A. L. Rowse (Ed.) WESTMINSTER ABBEY. 1972

Westminster Abbey is different things to different people.

To the *dévoué* it is the shrine containing the bones of its founder, St Edward the Confessor. Annual pilgrimages are made to it not only by members of the Church of England but by Roman Catholics, whose Cathedral is Bentley's magnificent basilica further down the road towards Victoria Station. For all the English it is the place where every monarch since William the Conqueror (except for Edward V and Edward VIII) has been consecrated with oil and crowned. For antiquaries it is Thorney Island. There are stone vestiges of St Edward the Confessor's original Saxon Abbey. For architects the present church and its great octagonal Chapter House are an exemplar of the Gothic style. Here in Nave, Transept and Cloister is the tall French architecture of the reign of Henry III when England was an integral part of Christendom. It is purest Early English, started in 1376* and continuing to be used in the building of the Nave until 1528, a remarkable survival of a strong plain style triumphing over fashion. At the east end is the last exuberant Tudor outburst of Gothic in Henry VII's Chapel, fan-vaulted English Perpendicular within, sheltering elaborate early Renaissance coloured monuments and gilded ironwork. Outside from across the Thames, Henry VII's Chapel must have looked like an elaborate galleon, for its pinnacles were topped with little gold pennons and vanes.

To the boys of Westminster School 'up Abbey' means going to the Abbey for their school chapel. In it they have daily services. The monks who served St Peter's Abbey, which the Confessor founded, were Benedictines and a teaching order. Boys were first taught by the monks, it is said, in the Western Cloister. There was also a grammar school west of the Abbey in the precincts. Queen Elizabeth I refounded the two schools as a single institution which is the present Westminster School. The Dean is *ex officio* Chairman of its Governors. In the Abbey at Coronations its scholars have the right to acclaim the monarch first. In the eighteenth century it was the greatest public school in England, and it is still one of them. For those interested in monumental sculpture the Abbey is

---

*1376 was the date the building of the Nave was started but not the date of the start of the Abbey. The rebuilding of the church itself was started in 1245 by Henry III, continuing the Lady Chapel built earlier and now replaced by the new Lady Chapel of Henry VII.

unrivalled in the kingdom. It has the handsomest tombs of every age from the medieval to the present. To the liturgiologist the services of the Abbey and its customs make it a unique survival. The late minor Canon and Sacrist, Jocelyn Perkins, wrote three volumes for the Alcuin Club on Westminster Abbey, its worship and ornaments (1938–52). The Dean, Canons, minor Canons, and Sacrist in their enviable houses about the precincts are the successors of the Benedictine monks. The surveyor, organist, vergers, masons and those concerned with the fabric are the equivalent of the lay-brothers of the medieval community.

For historians it is the burial place of our kings, queens, courtiers, statesmen, lawyers, writers, generals and particularly admirals and naval officers. Though one could not say that the poets buried in Poets' Corner run the whole gamut of Palgrave's *Golden Treasury*, they are a memorable group.

Joseph Addison in a paper to the *Spectator* for Friday 30 March 1711 said:

Upon going into the Church, I entertained myself with the digging of a Grave; and saw in every Shovel-full of it that was thrown up, the Fragment of a Bone or Skull intermixt with a kind of fresh mouldering Earth that some time or other had a place in the Composition of an human Body. Upon this, I began to consider with myself what innumerable Multitudes of People lay confused together under the Pavement of that ancient Cathedral; how Men and Women, Friends and Enemies, Priests and Soldiers, Monks and Prebendaries, were crumbled amongst one another, and blended together in the same common Mass; how Beauty, Strength, and Youth, with Old-age, Weakness, and Deformity, lay undistinguished in the same promiscuous Heap of Matter.

Or there was Max Beerbohm's essay on the Abbey's wax effigies, 'The Ragged Regiment' from *Yet Again* (1909).

Certainly, such of us as reside in London take Westminster Abbey as a matter of course. A few of us will be buried in it, but meanwhile we don't go to it, even as we don't go to the Tower, or the Mint, or the Monument. Only for some special purpose do we go – as to hear a sensational bishop preaching, or to see a monarch anointed. And on these rare occasions we cast but a casual glance at the Abbey – that close packed chaos of beautiful things and worthless vulgar things. That the Abbey should be thus chaotic does not seem strange to us; for lack of orderliness and discrimination is an essential characteristic of English genius. But to the Frenchman, with his passion for symmetry and harmony, how very strange it must all seem!

I suppose I was five when I first saw it. At that age there was the impression that it was only the South Transept. For most visitors, until recently, this was the chief entrance open to the public. One glanced in, the crowds were great, the place was tall and dark and surprisingly short for something so tall. I did not walk as far as the tower-crossing nor did I look down the Nave nor up to those three exquisite arches behind the High Altar. It was not until I was nine or ten that I was taken to the royal tombs and Henry VII's Chapel. These did not seem as interesting to me then as the Tower of London and Traitor's Gate. There were not enough ghosts. In those days I did not know that the bodies of Cromwell's government had been disinterred at the Restoration and thrown into a deep pit outside the Abbey and their decapitated heads displayed over Westminster Hall. I thought that anything really old and to be revered, had to be round-arched and Norman. As for the kings and tombs and effigies, they were a spate of words of vergers or schoolmasters or guides and too many to be taken in.

At the age of sixteen or seventeen one reacts against the opinions of one's parents. Mine admired the Gothic and the Abbey particularly, because it was Gothic and historic, two qualities of perfection. I was already tending towards the Georgian and had begun to admire the Baroque sculpture of Roubilliac and the pioneer investigation by Mrs Esdaile of eighteenth-century monuments. Partly to annoy my parents and old-fashioned schoolmasters, and also partly within myself, I then preferred St Paul's. When I came to work in London, after the usual two-year period of teaching in preparatory schools, my friend John Edward Bowle, the historian, had been made sixth-form history master at Westminster School. Thus I was able to discover the Armoury and the Little Cloister with its splashing fountain and its unforgettable view of Barry's Victoria Tower. I also discovered the Main Cloisters. As to the Canons and clergy, I knew none of them; they seemed to me semi-royal. The precincts of the Abbey, though they are blessedly open during most of the day, still have a forbiddingly private look.

As a journalist on the *Architectural Review* in Queen Anne's Gate, I found the Abbey a dominating presence. Those two Western Towers completed by Nicholas Hawksmoor, in his own version of Gothic, were to be seen every day down Tothill Street. A reproach to them, we modernists must have felt, was Charles Holden's London Transport Building, built in 1929, with its plain square tower in the latest modern unadorned functional style, and carved insets by Henry Moore, Eric Gill and others. This seemed the true Gothic. All the same there was the deeper call of the truer Gothic, when all ten bells rolled out on state occasions and when the lesser smaller melodious ring could be heard after fashionable weddings in St Margaret's.

In those days the interior of the Abbey was dark and dingy. The great Lethaby seemed to have concentrated on keeping the structure standing, and I have been told that his only artistic contribution was the rather inadequate brass electroliers. There were many things for a forward-looking architectural journalist to criticise. For instance the lettering on the Unknown Warrior's grave seemed a very long way from Eric Gill. It still seems so, and must have come from a monumental mason and been ordered by the foot and acquiesced in by the Dean and Chapter, who were only interested in the wording. But now I do not know that art is all that important in an inspired idea like this. In a way, this famous slab typifies the Abbey and that touch of the commonplace and the numinous which make it different from anywhere else.

Since the war the Abbey has been transformed inside and has flowered. The new Surveyor, Stephen Dykes Bower (appointed in 1951), first cleaned the stone and we realised that the grey Purbeck of the Henry III columns was designed to contrast with the cream-coloured Caen stone. The paintings on the vaulted roof became visible, including arabesques designed by Wren around the bosses. The early Renaissance monuments were startlingly restored to their full colour, which brought back the swagger and delightful vulgarity of the New Learning. The monument to Henry Carey, 1st Baron Hunsdon, in St John the Baptist's Chapel off the north ambulatory, must be the biggest in any church in England. The cleaning of the walls showed up the splendour of the eighteenth-century glass, particularly that in the West Window. The noble, white marble statues of Georgian and Victorian days were cleaned.

The internal glory has been almost wholly restored, yet the heart of the Abbey, the shrine of its founder, is a caricature of a shrine. It was despoiled in 1540, and though the relics are still inside it, the mosaics have been picked out from the stonework and its columns damaged. All this could easily be restored to what it was like when Henry III rebuilt the shrine. The Cosmati work with which it was adorned could be put back by modern craftsmen.

One of the first of the Victorian restorers of the Abbey was Edward Blore, who designed the Choir Screen in 1834. Greatly daring, the present Surveyor applied full colour to this screen and to the stalls within the Choir, which had later been restored by Sir Gilbert Scott, whose masterpiece is the restored Chapter House. This lightening of the former dinginess of the Abbey shows up how good Victorian work can be. Its proportions and detail are emphasised by bright-coloured paint and they are well suited to their surroundings, as is the restored stained glass in the Chapter House. Let us hope that this book will bring about the completion of the interior restoration of the Abbey. For the floors of Nave and Transepts, at present of inferior Portland stone, should be of more durable material, such as marble, to withstand the onslaught of thousands of shoes.

The chief delight of Westminster Abbey for the Londoner can be its daily services. I remember with embarrassment some satirical verses I

wrote before the war on official religion connected with the Abbey. After the war, when I deteriorated into becoming a committee man, I sat on a Commission whose offices were close by. After these painful and often boring sessions, it was a relief to come out into the open air. More often than not the two bells were ringing for Evensong, then I would go in to the service and be ushered into a seat near the Choir. The evening light would fade from the stained glass. Softened electric light threw mysterious shadows. The well-known prayer-book phrases were read by priests in canopied stalls. An anthem by Lawes or Weelkes or some

A 19th-century view of the outside of the Cloisters, seen also on the previous page

unrecognised Victorian musician soared to the vaulting. The Commission and the arguments fell into proportion and ceased to irritate. The traffic roar in Parliament Square, the 11s and the 24s, were muffled by the buttressed building. Even more than state occasions and memorial services, these weekday Evensongs have impressed me. The Abbey is more of an ancient abbey still at an 8 a.m. Communion Service in one of the side chapels, with only a few there.

For the purpose of writing this introduction, I was taken a final tour of the place by the Archdeacon, Canon Carpenter. It was a summer evening after the church had been shut. I walked to his house just as the gas-lights were being turned on in the Cloisters and cobbled passages of the royal surroundings of the Abbey. I was in the London of Dickens. As we passed the Chapter House, I remarked on how strange it was that this building, so well restored by Sir Gilbert Scott, was in the care of the Department of the Environment, and not of the Dean and Chapter. He pointed out that it had been the scene of the first English Parliament in the Royal Palace of Westminster and that it represented what the Abbey stands for, the tension between the present and the past. As we came into the Nave by the South-West Door, someone was playing the organ. There was a lay brother (i.e. a verger) on duty. The stained glass in the West Window, gold, blue, dark red and silver was at its Georgian armorial grandest. I saw the point of those crystal chandeliers, which were presented to the Abbey by the Guinness family after the last war. The lay brother turned them on and they gradually swelled in brightness, though there was never a glare. We walked round the tombs, up to St Edward's shrine, over the engineer's new bridge leading to it. This is as inoffensive as it is practical. We went into Henry VII's Chapel, and had a look at the praying hands of Margaret Beaufort. The lights were turned down into semi-darkness as we came out into the gas-lit mystery of the Cloister and past the Hall of Westminster School close by the Deanery – that Hall inside looks like a Georgian aquatint of the hall of a Cambridge College.

As I write these final sentences in a City of London precinct near the Norman church of Rahere's Priory of St Bartholomew the Great, the Corporation of London dust-cart is making a hellish noise under my window. There is always a tension between the past and the present. In Westminster Abbey the tension for most of us is created by the thousands of tourists of all nations and faiths who queue, apparently without comprehension, through a place which means much to us. But do they not understand? I think they do. Their shuffling presence remains after the doors are shut. Finally, at the south end of the South Transept hidden away, is the chapel of St Faith. This is for me the part of the Abbey where tension between past and present ceases.

St Mary Magdalen,
Old Fish Street Hill

On winter evenings I walk alone in the City
   When cobbles glisten with wet and it's foggy and still;
I am Rector's warden here. But more's the pity
   We haven't the Charity children now to fill
Our old west gallery front. Some new committee
   Has done away with them all. I beg your pardon,
   I omitted to tell you where I am Rector's warden —
At St Mary Magdalen's church, Old Fish Street Hill.

Unfortunately, the London Conflagration
   Of sixteen sixty-six was a moment when
The Roman style in general estimation
   Was held so high that our church was rebuilt by Wren.
It is a just a box with a fanciful plaster ceiling
Devoid of a vestige of genuine Christian feeling,
   And our congregation is seldom more than ten.*

*Demolished in 1886.

Old St Pancras Church

BALLET. NOVEMBER 1951

Old St Pancras Church, where Marie Taglioni was married to Comte Gilbert de Voisins on 14 July 1832, and where Joseph Grimaldi the dancing clown was wed, is hooted at by railways, swished past by trolley-buses, shaken by lorries, deafened by drays, smoked out by gas works, and now, at the time of writing, frowned upon by two cliffs of neo-moderne borough council flats which are nearly complete. The Midland rolls into its Gothic terminus to the east, beyond that the Great Northern gets up steam for Cleethorpes. Behind where you are sitting in the picture, the London & North Western is making itself felt. What you are looking at is a parish church in the Anglo-Norman style of 1840, encasing and overwhelming what was once an ancient, dim little Middlesex fane not unlike Perivale, Northolt or Ickenham.

In the churchyard outside, which is half sooty municipal garden and too cemeterial for a nice progressive reccy-ground, lies the great late Georgian architect Sir John Soane. The tomb is of his own design, enormous and in his strange Soanean classic style, which has so much influenced modern Scandinavian architecture.

The church inside has been altered by bombing which smashed the Victorian stained glass windows. Now the glass is clear. Sooty thorns show through the east window. The interior walls have been whitened, the floors sensitively renewed with wood blocks and huge grave slabs of slate and stone. An altar stone, said to have been dedicated by St Augustine in 602, has been dug out of a wall of the church and replaced on the high altar. The Victorian iron screen has been gilded, and very nice it looks. There is decoration in the style of the late Martin Travers. The Blessed Sacrament is here, so it is an easy church for praying. It is a core of quiet in the noise of transport. The ironwork entrance gate is mostly eighteenth-century, removed I suppose, from some merchant's country house in the parish. And inside the church with the monuments of these seventeenth and eighteenth century citizens looking down from the white walls, it is easy to be back in the days when this was St Pancras-in-the-Fields and people came to be wedded or were carried to the font or a hole in the earth, from a newly built stucco box or older brown brick Middlesex farm.

St. Mary-le-Strand

A letter to THE TIMES. 5 NOVEMBER 1981

Sir, The threatened loss of St. Mary-le-Strand is
calamitous. It was a chapel dedicated to our Lord
on the north bank of the Thames. It was designed by a
Scottish architect, James Gibbs, and completed in 1717;
it looks like a grotto inside and its outside is
familiar to all Londoners from the cover of *Strand
Magazine*. What money can compensate for the loss of
so familiar and loved a building?

Yours faithfully,   John Betjeman
                                         Osbert Lancaster

St. Mary-le-Strand

Published as a broadsheet in 1981

Shall we give Gibbs the go by
Great Gibbs of Aberdeen,
Who gave the town of Cambridge
Its Senate House serene;
And every son of Oxford
Can recognise he's home
When he sees upon the skyline
The Radcliffe's mothering dome.
Placid above the chimney pots
His sculptured steeples soar,
Windowless he designs his walls
Above the traffic's roar.
Whenever you put stone on stone
You edified the scene,
Your chaste baroque was on its own,
Great Gibbs of Aberdeen.
A Tory and a Catholic
There's nothing quite so grand
As the baroque of your Chapel
Of St. Mary in the Strand.*

*Restored 1985–7.

Church of the Ark of the Covenant

SPECTATOR. 3 FEBRUARY 1956

I had the unspeakable privilege this week of going inside the Church of the Ark of the Covenant on Clapton Common, E5. Many a time have I stood outside those barricaded *art nouveau* railings and looked up at the soaring stone spire, with great bronze beasts at its base, and regarded that locked door with longing. I have imagined those days in 1895 when Clapton was a leafy suburb and carriage folk lived in the wide Italianate roads and the church was built by those who believed that the Reverend J. H. Smyth-Pigott was the Son of God. For only six years did the church remain open and after that the believers, with their leader, retired to the Agapemone, or Abode of Love, at Spaxton in Somerset, where some of them still survive. They were good, gentle people, much maligned. Certainly the inside of their church at Clapton is a blaze of glory. The stone altar with a carved chair behind it gleams white below the gold mosaic of the sanctuary. But the wonder of the church is the stained glass, highly coloured flowers, birds and fishes and trailing figures all designed by Walter Crane and executed by Silvester Sparrow. It is the richest Victorian glass I have ever seen and makes Burne-Jones and Rossetti look pale by comparison. Clapton has changed its character since those days when the handsome Messiah and his Brides and other followers knew it. It is more international. Blocks of council flats rise from the gardens of demolished Georgian houses. With a son of Smyth-Pigott I went to find where his father had lived. Only a cedar tree remained. The walled garden had become a garage and the site was occupied by modernistic flats. But the railway station, dear dark cavernous Great Eastern Clapton, is the same.*

*The church still stands in Rookwood Road, Clapton Common. Since 1956 it has been occupied by the Ancient Catholic Church who have renamed it the Church of the Good Shepherd.

Wood del.　　　　　　　　　　　　　　　　　J. C. Griffiths sc.

WILLESDEN CHURCH, MIDDLESEX.

In Willesden Churchyard

Come walk with me, my love, to Neasden Lane.
The chemicals from various factories
Have bitten deep into the Portland stone
And streaked the white Carrara of the graves
Of many a Pooter and his Caroline,
Long laid to rest among these dripping trees;
And that small heap of fast-decaying flowers
Marks Lupin Pooter lately gathered in;
And this, my love, is Laura Seymour's grave —
'So long the loyal counsellor and friend'
Of that Charles Reade whose coffin lies with hers.
Was she his mistress? Did he visit her
When coming down from Oxford by the coach?
Alighting at the turnpike, did he walk
These elmy lanes of Middlesex and climb
A stile or two across the dairy farms
Over to Harlesden at the wicket gate?
Then the soft rigours of his Fellowship
Were tenderly relaxed. The sun would send
Last golden streaks of mild October light
On tarred and weather-boarded barn and shed.
Blue bonfire smoke would hang among the trees;
And in the little stucco hermitage
Did Laura gently stroke her lover's head?
And did her Charles look up into her eyes
For loyal counsel there? I do not know.
Doubtless some pedant for his Ph.D.
Has ascertained the facts, or I myself
Might find them in the public libraries.
I only know that as we see her grave
My flesh, to dissolution nearer now
Than yours, which is so milky white and soft,
Frightens me, though the Blessed Sacrament
Not ten yards off in Willesden parish church
Glows with the present immanence of God.

St Dunstan, Stepney

SPECTATOR. 15 FEBRUARY 1957

One of the most repulsive forms of Subtopia is the current fashion for turning old country churchyards into semi-recreation grounds. A fate like this awaits one of the most remarkable and attractive Georgian country churchyards I know, and oddly enough it is in East London. It is that of the old parish church of St Dunstan, Stepney. Extensive bombing has turned the area beyond the churchyard into open country littered with prefabs. When the area comes to be rebuilt it should be possible for the LCC to create plenty of open space while keeping the churchyard the countrified place it is and retaining undisturbed the clustered Portland-stone Georgian headstones of various elegant outlines and commemorating dead merchants and sea captains as the charming and essential foreground they are to the old church. Perhaps it is not too late to suggest this, and St Dunstan's will be the first churchyard in London to be treated as something of beauty and not merely as something of antiquarian interest or a crazy-paved 'garden of rest'.*

*The churchyard is still a countrified place. Flats have replaced the prefabs around it.

THE THAMES

At Richmond

Blackfriars

By the shot tower
  near the chimneys
Off the road to
  Waterloo
Stands the cottage
  of 'The Ancient'
As in eighteen-
  forty two.
Over brickwork,
  brownish brickwork
Lilac hangs in
  London sun
And by light fan-
  tastic clockwork
Moves the drawbridge
  sounds the gun.
When the sunset
  in the side streets
Brought the breezes
  up the tide

Floated bits of
  daily journals
Stable smells and
  silverside.
And the gaslight
  yellow gaslight
Flaring in its
  wiry cage,
Like the Prison
  Scene in *Norval*
On the old Ol-
  ympic stage,
Lit the archway
  as the thunder
And the rumble
  and the roll
Heralded a
  little handcart
And 'The Ancient'
  selling coal.

Rotherhithe

DAILY TELEGRAPH. 7 OCTOBER 1963

When my rooms in the City of London were damaged by fire, a friend offered me accommodation in Rotherhithe, a seafaring village on the South Bank, down stream from London Bridge. It has an eighteenth-century church and school and a public house licensed to sell stamps as well as beer and spirits.

The house in Rotherhithe Street where I lived was in a row whose irregular two-storey street façade was, as it still is, rundown-looking for lack of a lick of paint. But inside, the house, like its neighbours, was a revelation. It had eighteenth-century panelled rooms, humble and uneven and put there by some merchant captain in the days of Tom Bowling. Best of all, my bedroom hung over the Thames, with a tremendous view. Up-stream I could see the dome of St Paul's framed in the silhouette of Tower Bridge. Down-stream I looked towards the masts, funnels and cranes of the Pool of London. On the opposite bank were the wharves and Georgian brick buildings of Wapping.

The air was always fresh and with a hint of the sea in it. At night, with the lights reflecting in the water, the scene was equally enthralling. Passing craft were a continual interest. I put my bed on the river side of the room and it was delicious to go to sleep to the solacing sounds of water. At low tide there would be the distant chug of a passing tug and a few seconds later the swish of the waves caused by her wake rippling over the pebbles and mud below my window. At high tide after a tug had passed the water made a plopping sound right against my bedroom wall as though I were in a ship's hold.

It was the most restful few months I had ever spent in London. The people of Rotherhithe were a friendly village with a life of their own. Taking a ticket to London from that obscure Underground station at the southern opening of Sir Marc Brunel's Thames Tunnel was like setting off from home into a stranger land.

It struck me then that houses hanging over water are the ideal antidote to the noise and diesel fumes of modern big cities. Here are sites with quiet and fresh air. Being on the actual bank of the river the houses are dry and propped up well above tide level. It amazes me that no planner has yet had the imagination to build houses in the gaps along the bombed sites of London's South Bank or to adapt as flats parts of the wharves along the City shore.

These charming old houses at Rotherhithe, now owned by the LCC and so delightful and comfortable to live in, are the only examples surviving the whole way up the South Bank until you reach Mortlake, in Surrey. All other houses facing the Thames are rendered noisy by thundering roads between them and the river. The sad thing about the old houses at Rotherhithe is that instead of being added to, they are to be destroyed by the LCC which owns them, despite continued and vigorous protests from those who live in them.* Though they are in excellent repair inside, they used not to be considered of architectural importance when the Ministry lists were made. They are just 'buildings' like most houses in England – your house probably and certainly mine – lived in by those of us still allowed to live on the ground and not in blocks of flats. Admittedly they are older and more picturesque than any other London riverside group of houses.

*The houses in Rotherhithe Street were destroyed in the late 1960s.

The Tunnel at Wapping

SPECTATOR. 19 JULY 1957

I went lately to the isolated East London village of Wapping for the centenary celebrations of the famous church of St Peter's, London Docks. The Underground station at Wapping is the most interesting and historic on the whole London Transport system. From its narrow platform you can see into the Thames Tunnel with its brick arches just as they were in 1824 when Sir Marc Brunel, the father of an even greater son, first designed them. I learn from L. T. C. Rolt's interesting biography of the son, I. K. Brunel, that Marc conceived the idea of how to build this, the first sub-acqueous tunnel in the world, from watching the tunnelling action of the ship worm *teredo navalis* in ships' timbers while he was working in Chatham dockyard. He constructed the Tunnel by building a shield in the form of six massive cast-iron frames which were divided into three storeys and each storey consisting of twelve cells in which excavators worked. The excavators dug out to a depth of four and a half inches so that the shield moved four and half inches at a time. The process took years because of flooding and lack of money. But today, if you stand at the river end of Wapping Station, you can see the light from Rotherhithe shining on the rails at the other end as the tunnel dips down under the bed of the river.

London's Bridges

(It seems probable that this article was never published though it may have appeared in the *Daily Telegraph* or *Telegraph Weekend Magazine*.)

There are twenty-five bridges over the Thames between the Tower of London and Twickenham. Eight are of cast iron and carry railways. The remaining seventeen are of varying materials – stone, cast iron, and concrete, in that chronological order – and carry roads. Pilots of tugs carry the diminishing barge traffic above London Bridge. They and the summer visitors on steamers are almost the only people who look at the bridges. To most Londoners, the bridges are a gap between the houses on the diesel-laden journey between north and south, some affording views of the once famous and now blocked-out City skyline.

Hard though it is to imagine it today, London must be thought of as built first on islands in a marsh either side of a slow-flowing, winding river. Two of the steepest near the river bank are Cornhill and Ludgate Hill, between which the Walbrook flows, and these are the City of London. West of it the Fleet river, once so named for its rapidity, joins the Thames. Streams from Middlesex uplands, of which the best known is the Westbourne, create a marsh round Thorney Island on which stands Westminster Abbey. Those Saxon suffixes, '-ey' and '-ea', signifying islet, denote other islands in the marsh where habitations could be built: Stepney, Bermondsey, Chelsea, Battersea, Putney.

This wide, flat river scene, far from stone quarries, did not lend itself at first to more than wooden bridges. Nor were bridges needed. One was enough for London, which had been a fortified city since Roman times, the river protecting its south side, and stone walls with gates the remaining sides. The first stone London bridge was not built until the reign of Henry II (1154–89) and replaced a wooden one. It stood east of the present structure (designed by John Rennie and his son, 1823–31, and widened in 1904) and its eastern footwalk was entered under the tower of St Magnus-the-Martyr Church House and a chapel stood above its many arches. A seventeenth-century engraving shows the heads of traitors impaled on pikes over the Southwark gateway. The arches acted as a sluice against incoming tides at low water. The upper river poured with a roar under the houses on the bridge and daring watermen used to shoot the rapids.

Old prints and paintings show the Thames above the bridge as full of shipping. Sailing barges brought hay, grain and stone from as far upstream as Oxfordshire to Queenhythe. The London Thames, much broader and clearer than now, flecked with brightly coloured shipping whose masts and sails were seen from the Surrey bank against a forest of church towers and steeples, each with a gilded vane, around St Paul's, must have been one of the most entrancing sights of Europe. And so it was again, after the Fire of 1666, when it was rebuilt in dark red, Dutch-looking brick, and Wren's white stone and black lead steeples and towers led the eye to the first storey and to the dome of his new cathedral.

People did not think of bridges across the Thames as architecture until the eighteenth century. Besides that, the watermen of London did not want to lose their living. There were a few wooden bridges between Surrey and Middlesex banks, one at Putney, another at Kew and the wooden bridge at Battersea survived long enough to be the subject of some of Whistler's romantic etchings and paintings.

Times grew safer. City merchants set up as country squires in outlying villages. In 1758 London Bridge was widened and the houses either side of it demolished, but the medieval arches remained. The first bridge to be rebuilt with a view to elegance as well as function, was that at West-minster. It was of stone and rose steeply in the middle and had round arches between piers crowned with dome-like stone tops at parapet level, and was designed in 1750 by a Swiss engineer, Charles Labalye. It was demolished in 1857 and rebuilt, wider and flatter with Gothic cast iron arches and Gothic stone piers ending in iron Gothic gas lamp standards, all from the design of the engineer Thomas Page, in collaboration with Sir Charles Barry, the architect of the Houses of Parliament.

In 1760 the Scottish architect, Robert Mylne, prepared designs for a stone bridge at Blackfriars, which was flatter and more graceful than that at Westminster, and which had coupled columns adorning the piers. It was demolished in 1863, when Joseph Cubitt, the engineer, erected the present Gothic bridge, with cast iron arches and piers of polished Aberdeen granite. In 1789, James Paine, the architect of many noblemen's houses and stables, replaced the old bridge at Kew with a high arched one in stone, since demolished to make way for more traffic.

This was the time when London was spreading, roads improving and carriages were faster and lighter. Citizens were ceasing to live in the City over their place of business, and coming in for work by day. The poet Cowper describes the Georgian houses near London in, as it was, Kennington:

> Tight boxes, neatly sashed, and all ablaze
> To catch the midday sun's united rays,
> Delight the citizen, who, gasping there,
> Breathes clouds of dust and calls it country air.

There was a move from the City to South London, the leafy heights of Camberwell, to the drained fields round Brixton, Peckham and Stockwell, and even as far out as Clapham Common.

Old Waterloo Bridge, 1923

A short way from South London to the newly fashionable West End was through Vauxhall. In 1811, John Rennie, the Scottish architect-engineer (these were the days before civil engineering and architecture were professionally separated) built the first cast iron bridge to be seen in London at Vauxhall. The piers between the arches, however, were of granite. It was demolished in 1906 for the present bridge, a fine piece of architecture.

The same great bridge builder designed, in 1813, a new bridge faced with Cornish granite at Waterloo. It was long and flat, with nine semi-elliptic arches, with coupled Doric columns between them, and was considered by Canova to be the finest bridge in Europe. We, who remember it, can recall the perfect foreground it made to Somerset House, and distant views of the dome of St Paul's. On the Embankment side some of its nobly simple granite detail survives.

For not very convincing reasons about its safety and width, it was destroyed before the War, at the instance of Lord Morrison of Lambeth, then chairman of the LCC, and the present structure, by Rendel Palmer and Tritton, with architectural treatment by Sir Giles Gilbert Scott, was erected in 1939–45. The new bridge, graceful in itself, because of its slight curve, is less satisfactory in the setting. Always, it is transport which changes the character and shape of a city. New structural materials speed the change. Already a road bridge of cast iron carried by chain suspension had been built by Brunel in 1841–5 across the Thames at Charing Cross. This was replaced by Sir John Hawkshaw's present Hungerford Railway Bridge in 1860–3, and the chains of the old bridge were used for Brunel's mighty suspension bridge across the Avon gorge at Clifton. The first railway to cross the Thames to London was the Brighton line at Pimlico and Jacomb Hood's cast iron bridge there (1859, and since widened) was built in fifteen months.

Railways invaded the City from the south, in 1863, at Cannon Street and Blackfriars; between 1862 and 1864 Joseph Cubitt and F. T. Turner adorned their railway bridge at Blackfriars with cast iron emblems of the London, Chatham and Dover – the London, Smash 'em and Turnover, as it used to be called. The West London extension crossed from Clapham to Kensington in 1863 and already the London and South-western had come in over the Thames at Barnes (1849) and Kew (1863). It crossed at Putney in 1878.

London had spread so far into Surrey, Kent and Middlesex that road bridges, as well as railways, had to be built to take the clerks and their wives from the new suburbs of south London into the metropolis, in the age of steam, hansom cabs and horse buses. Companies were formed to build toll bridges. Thomas Page built a splendid oriental style suspension bridge at Chelsea, which was planned in 1846 but, owing to financial troubles, not finished until 1863. It was grimly simplified and rebuilt in 1934. R. W. Ordish's delightfully fantastic Albert Bridge (1873) luckily still survives. It is not a true suspension bridge. Its road is carried by diagonal bars from the towers on the same principle Ordish had already employed at Moldau, over the Danube.

The most loved London bridge, the Tower, was engineered by Sir John Wolf Barry, and its architect was Sir Horace Jones. It shows the importance of skyline. Sir Horace's chief draughtsman at this time was a follower of Pugin and the father of Sir Frank Brangwyn, and this may account for the rather Flemish Gothic of the bridge, as well as its sense of outline. The idea of a bascule bridge at this point is attributed to Sir Horace Jones, the City architect who designed Smithfield and Leadenhall Markets.

The man who changed London rivers more than any other was Sir Joseph Bazalgette (1819–91) the son of a Commander in the Royal Navy, of French extraction. His portrait in the Institution of Mechanical Engineers shows a small man with bald head and large moustache. There is a medallion of him on the Victoria Embankment which he designed. He was asthmatic and retiring and is buried in Wimbledon Parish Churchyard, having begotten children, designed three bridges, Putney

(1884), Hammersmith suspension (1884–7, replacing a Greek suspension bridge of 1827) and Battersea (1886–90), and saved London from plague.

From the Middle Ages until the 1840s, the stink of sewage, much of which flowed down the tributary streams, particularly the Fleet, which was mostly ordure, dead dogs and rubbish, had caused disease. Sir Joseph planned the scheme whereby the sewage was carried by eighty-three miles of pipes eastward down the north bank to Barking and down the south bank to Crossness. The tributary rivers were bricked over and used only to carry away the rainwater from London's roofs and pavements. The extra rush of water after storms meant embanking the Thames and raising all wharves above flood level, which is why there are no picturesque old wharves along the Thames today and why its waters do not lap under the arches of Somerset House nor fill the moat of the Tower. Only the river Wandle, through Wandsworth, and the Stamford Brook from Acton were still used for sewage.

There was a reaction in the present century against the gaunt cast iron constructions of the civil engineers, even though Bazalgette had let himself go in his picturesque reconstruction of Hammersmith suspension bridge. Architects were called in to make new bridges genteel. Sir Ernest George, a scholarly country house architect to rich Edwardians, designed Southwark Bridge in a Renaissance style in 1915. When Peter Barlow's gaunt suspension bridge at Lambeth (1862) was declared unsafe, Sir Reginald Blomfield was called in to add architecture to the new one in 1932. By now, concrete was the usual material for road bridges. Nevertheless, Sir Herbert Baker in 1933 added stone balusters to the new bridge at Chiswick and only at Twickenham is there a new concrete bridge (1933).

For a picturesque effect, my own favourite bridges are the Tower, Albert and Hammersmith. For structural adornment, Blackfriars, Westminster and Vauxhall; and for simplicity, Twickenham. But they will never be looked at with pleasure until less sewage comes down from upstream and until the outfalls of Sir Joseph's sewer pipes are moved nearer to the sea.

The Romance of the Thames

SPECTATOR. 7 OCTOBER 1955

Chelsea Reach and Lots Road Power Station

I stood last Sunday afternoon in the warm October sunlight with a beautiful girl beside me on Battersea Bridge. The high tide was just ebbing out, and as we looked down into the filthy brown water the refuse became so embarrassing that I had to suggest we walked on into Battersea. In the silence which followed the contemplation of the sliding train of filthy intimate objects we had seen, I realised that the Thames water in London is incurably disgusting. Presumably the filth floats up through London from drains in the neighbourhod of Barking Creek on the incoming tide. It reaches Teddington and by that time is ready to slide down to Barking on the outward tide. So it goes backwards and forwards through the middle of London until time and tide dissolve it. We walked round to Battersea Church and the arid little park beyond it, where some plane trees and ill-kept grass border the Thames. The water here was more stagnant and floating sticks in it stirred up clouds of brown revolving dirt. Although it was a fine Sunday afternoon, we could understand why this little park was empty. The stench was overwhelming. On whom does the responsibility for the purification of this tidal water fall? On the Thames Conservancy? On the Port of London Authority? On the London County Council?

PUBLIC BUILDINGS

London River's Gothic Crown

DAILY TELEGRAPH. 14 MAY 1957

Whatever we may think of our Member, we all admire the Houses of Parliament. The angry constituent, coming up to attack his MP, is awed by the majesty of the Strangers' Entrance, silenced by the cavernous splendour of Westminster Hall and the broad ascent and corridor of St Stephen's Hall with its paintings and vaulting and statues. He feels himself the inheritor of a thousand years of government and that he is one with the Kings and statesmen whose figures are portrayed around him. There in the vaulted Central Hall, that handsome octagon with its branching chandelier, is his MP, dwarfed to insignificance by his surroundings and coming forward over the coloured Minton tiles to meet him.

MPs show constituents round in one of two moods. They either affect to be unimpressed by the Gothic corridors, rich book-cases, red carpets and gleaming armorial glass – 'all this money wasted on decoration should have been given to the poor: besides, it's a fake' (pause for false modesty) 'like we all are.' Alternatively they may be determined to impress the visitor with the wonder of the British Constitution – every ceremony will be described, every doorknob and framed relic will be examined, everything will be thought centuries old.

The truth is that no one can be indifferent to the Houses of Parliament. Inside and outside, this Royal Palace of Westminster is great architecture. It has weathered all phases of criticism. By the time it was finished in 1860, the sort of Gothic in which it was built was quite out of fashion. People thought its Tudor style 'debased'. The Law Courts in the Strand (1868–82) represented popular taste. Yet as Norman Shaw, the architect of Scotland Yard, remarked, 'as a faithful reproduction of Gothic the Law Courts are far superior to the Houses of Parliament, but somehow or other the latter are more adapted to modern requirements.' In our own age it has been fashionable until lately to despise all decoration on buildings as something immoral, unhygienic and dust-collecting. On the Houses of Parliament, inside and out, there is hardly a square foot of undecorated space.

On mugs and jugs and Treasury notes, in film and plastic and paint, the famous outline has been reproduced thousands of times. But though everyone knows the building, few know about its architect, Sir Charles

Barry, and his helper A. W. N. Pugin. On the night of 16 October 1834, Charles Barry, the architect son of a Westminster stationer, was returning by coach from Brighton when he saw the glow of a great fire on the London side of the river. All the Houses of Parliament, a clutter of buildings of various dates, were destroyed; only Westminster Hall and the crypt of St Stephen's Chapel remained. There was a competition to rebuild the Houses, and owing to the antiquity of the site and the proximity of the Abbey, competitors were asked to produce a Gothic design. Now Barry was a classic man. He had already designed the City Art Gallery, Manchester, and the much admired Travellers' Club, Pall Mall. His chief Gothic buildings had been the King Edward VI School, Birmingham (now destroyed) and the new St Peter's church on the Steyne at Brighton. He won the Houses of Parliament competition out of ninety-seven entries through the brilliance of his plan, which retained Westminster Hall and made it a feature of one entrance.

The chief parts of the building – the octagon and the vaulted corridors which lead from it to the Commons on one side and to the Lords on the other – are hidden from the public streets. A separate Royal entrance under Victoria Tower leads through the Robing Room and magnificent Royal Gallery to the Lords. Along the river front are libraries, with the Speaker's House and the Lord Chancellor's house on either corner. Offices face the Abbey and Victoria Gardens. The sort of building Barry liked was an oblong with a high tower at the corner. Hence the positions of the Victoria Tower and Big Ben. He also liked his corners to be filled in. He preferred Italian palaces to old English houses, and for the river front he seized the chance to make a symmetrical façade of classic proportions but with Gothic details. This caused his friend Pugin to exclaim 'all Greek' as he went past in a boat on the river. On the other fronts Barry made a deliberately irregular design.

In 1844 he put Pugin, who had helped him over the King Edward VI School at Birmingham, in charge of all metal work, wood carving and stained glass, with instructions that the style must be Tudor and the outside decoration as much as possible like that on Henry VII's Chapel, Westminster Abbey. Pugin was a convinced medievalist, a convert to Rome, a sailor, a humorist and a true artist. It is his work which gives the details of the interior such distinction. I think it probable, too, that Pugin devised the gables on the outside, and he may have been responsible for the effective way in which the clock stage of the Big Ben Tower projects beyond the stonework below. Certainly the linen-fold panelling, door plates, brass chandeliers, flock papers and carved fireplaces are all his; and the rich colours, red, brown and gold, have a Pugin look.

Pugin died insane in 1852 at the age of forty. Barry in that year was knighted, and died in 1860, aged sixty-five. After their deaths the families of the architects quarrelled, and it has been the custom to take sides. If you are a Puginite you must make out that Barry was a clever business man who took all the credit. Barry's other works alone should prove that this is not true. The building is clearly the result of what is known to have been an amicable partnership, with Barry as architect and Pugin as chief decorator.

During the last war the House of Commons was bombed. It has been rebuilt in 'utility Gothic'; this compares unfavourably with the House of Lords, which mercifully still has the Pugin decorations. Other bombed parts of the building, including restaurants and committee rooms, have unfortunately been restored internally in a style like that of an hotel lounge of twenty years ago – brown and beige and shiny.

The Duke of York's Column

SPECTATOR. 14 DECEMBER 1956 & 18 JANUARY 1957

What is Auntie *Times* up to, advocating the destruction of the Duke of York's column in Carlton House Terrace, as she did in a leader last week? The column (1831–4) by Benjamin Dean Wyatt is a most beautifully proportioned monument designed for where it stands and carefully related in scale to Carlton House Terrace. Instead of being destroyed, it might well be cleaned, as the Duke of Wellington advocated a few years ago. Its base is of pale grey granite and the column itself of pale pink granite – you may see this if you go close to it on a sunny day – and the grey and pink washed would make a superb contrast with the creamy stucco of the Terrace, and the green of the plane trees in the Mall. Auntie suggests that Nelson should have the monopoly of this part of the London sky, presumably because she prefers Nelson to the poor old Duke of York, whom she considers unworthy of her columns or any others. But Auntie is here discussing history and she should not confuse it with art. The Nelson column (1840–3) by W. Railton (lions 1867) is not related to its site and, to anyone who uses his eyes, it can hardly compare in dignity and scale with the York column.

Two correspondents have told me the same story about the Duke of York's column, and, as their accounts tally, I suppose there must be truth in it. One, an Oxford don, quotes the story as an illustration of the efficacy of a question in Parliament. Some time in the Fifties an old general descending the Duke of York's Steps, was almost ridden down by two tipsy subalterns galloping up them for a bet. A Parliamentary question followed, and to prevent a recurrence of the incident a sentry was placed there. Twenty years later, noticing that the sentry was getting wet, a soft-hearted MP asked another question and, as a result, an ironwork canopy was placed above him. Twenty years later, a retrenchment-minded MP asked a question about the waste of military manpower and the sentry was removed. Twenty years later, a tidy-minded MP asked a question about the rusting fragment of an iron canopy, and the Board of Works sent a man to saw it off. Today the rust stains remain, though the crevices have been filled with concrete. If the monument is cleaned, I hope two tipsy subalterns will ride down another general . . . long live the Constitution!

The Criterion Theatre

THE CONNOISSEUR. JANUARY 1974

Theatres are the most vulnerable of all public buildings. This is because almost invariably they occupy sites in the centres of towns and cities and on the whole are a financial risk to their owners. Developers have seized on them everywhere, pulled them down and sometimes, in the case of the Royalty Theatre, London, have included a small theatre in the new block as a gesture. Churches in towns are equally vulnerable. Here the developer is prepared to leave a prayer-room in a block of flats as a sop to God. The Criterion Theatre, Piccadilly Circus, was naturally threatened by developers in some of the schemes put forward. Sometimes there were face-saving gestures to the architecture of entertainment. It was largely due to the enterprise of Ian Albery of Wyndham Theatres Limited in the first place and his staff, and the theatrical profession and the Greater London Council Historic Buildings Section that the hand of the destroyer was restrained. Mr Ian Albery produced a coloured photograph of the very elegant interior of this theatre which is almost wholly underground. This he turned into a postcard which had printed on the back: 'Auditorium Criterion Theatre, Piccadilly Circus, London W.1. Architect – Thomas Verity – 1873, Proposed for demolition by Westminster City Council 1973'. All amenity societies and institutions connected with the theatrical profession used them as well as the present writer.

The Criterion Restaurant and Theatre is a statutory listed building 'As being of special architectural or historic interest'. Future intending developers will have to face a public enquiry if they wish to destroy either the Criterion Theatre or the Restaurant above. The Criterion was designed by Thomas Verity in 1871 and completed by 1873. It was the first multi-purpose restaurant in London and its promoters were the caterers, Spiers and Pond Ltd. Raymond Mander and Joe Mitcheson in their invaluable *Harvest Book of The Theatres of London*, say that the Criterion was originally to have been a concert-hall in the form of a square galleried room.

Thomas Verity, who died at his residence in Cathcart Road, South Kensington, in 1891, was an ingenious planner. He was a young man when he entered and won the competition for the building of a large tavern and restaurant on a plot of land sloping steeply northwards to Piccadilly and extending to Jermyn Street. Into this, his Criterion building, he packed a ballroom at the top, dining rooms in the middle and a theatre in the basement. The exterior with its mansard roofs and flanking projections was of Portland stone. This made it prominent in a

[166]

district which was mostly brick and stucco for it was at the edge of John Nash's grand scheme for linking Regent's Park to Carlton House and St James's Park by Regent's Street and Waterloo Place. This French intrusion into what was otherwise Greek or Roman-style architecture must have seemed out of place. But it redeemed itself by the elegance and simplicity of its main façade on Piccadilly. Its roofs were in mansard-form, a novelty for those times in London. The interiors, where they survive on the first floor of the restaurant building, are Frenchified elegance itself, the best of all being the banqueting hall in the centre of the building which looks out on to Piccadilly Circus.*

*The Criterion Theatre and Brasserie on the ground floor have been restored. However, controversy now surrounds the future of the extension (1878–9) as well as part of the original Verity building (1870–4) as permission has been granted to demolish this part of the site (bounded by 218–229 Piccadilly, the Haymarket and Jermyn Street) and replace the existing buildings with a vast new development.

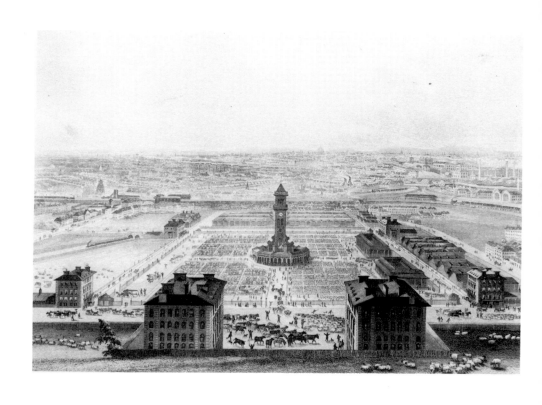

Caledonian Market

SPECTATOR. 10 MAY 1957

I was standing lately high above King's Cross in the airy, paved expanse of Copenhagen Fields, now known as the Metropolitan Cattle Market or Caledonian Market, Islington.* There in the centre is the tall Italianate tower with its sheds below. Far away to east and west the tall administrative buildings and the public houses are all part of the same scheme, designed by J. B. Bunning (1852–5). There was not a soul about. This splendid empty market belongs to the City of London. Now the frustrations of London traffic in its centre are as much to do with markets as anything else. Fruit lorries belonging to Covent Garden block up streets as far from their destination as St Martin's Lane, Garrick Street and Irving Street on the west. Smithfield blocks up a northern quarter of the City itself. Neither Leadenhall Market nor Billingsgate could be called conveniently situated, lost as they are among medieval lanes. Leadenhall and Covent garden would make charming shopping arcades in districts where shops are wanted. I have never heard the arguments in favour of retaining the markets on their present sites nor the arguments against moving Covent Garden, the most obstructive of them, to Islington. All I know is that when Herbert Morrison gleefully destroyed Rennie's masterpiece Waterloo Bridge in 1939 we were told that a wider bridge there would mean a direct north–south route through Central London. But Covent Garden is too firmly entrenched, it seems, for this to happen.

*The Caledonian Market closed at the outbreak of the First World War but it was not until 1965 that the buildings were destroyed, except for the taverns and central tower, and the land used for flats.

Columbia Market

SPECTATOR. 13 DECEMBER 1957

As the train draws in to Liverpool Street and before it sinks into the cutting look to your right. Rising above the chimney-pots is the most extravagant and benevolent fantasy in all London – Columbia Market.* Not even St Pancras Hotel excels it in picturesque outline and wealth of sculptured detail. The spires and pinnacles, the ironwork and stonework, black and silvery-white against the grey London sky, are like one of Pugin's dreams come true. Columbia Market was designed and built in 1866–8 from the designs of H. Alfred Darbishire for Baroness Burdett-Coutts to benefit the cheated artisans of Bethnal Green. The idea was that here honest dealing should go on without any swearing. It cost £200,000 even in those days and if you go in under the gate-house you will find a cloistered walk leading to a great market hall. The hall itself has granite columns supported by a vaulted wooden roof and lit by huge windows in the Decorated style. Here and there are carved Gothic inscriptions saying things like 'Speak every man truth with his neighbour', and among them the ladders, barrels, bricks and implements of the LCC housing department are stored. For the truth is that this glorious effort of Victorian philanthropy planned in the comfortable house of the millionairess was a failure from the start. Now I learn that the LCC is likely to demolish this remarkable building which could hardly be less fashionable nor more impressive. As Dr Pevsner says, 'the building should be preserved at all cost.' It seems hard to believe that in a district so lacking in distinguished architecture some use cannot be found, at any rate, for the hall, quadrangle and gate-house, or are we to have one more vertical slab with a horizontal slab alongside it to dominate this murky hilltop? Paint and imaginative reconstruction could transform Columbia Market into one of the glories of London.

*Columbia Market was demolished between 1958 and 1966 and the land used for housing.

The National Theatre

From a letter to Sir Denys Lasdun. 4 NOVEMBER 1973

Now I was anyhow going to write to you to tell you a moment of
exaltation I had. I was in a taxi with Osbert Lancaster last week on my
way to the City from County Hall. It was a fine crisp morning, blue sky
and a little mist about. As our cab crawled out of that hell hole they
have dug in front of Waterloo Bridge, I gasped with delight at the cube
of your theatre in the pale blue sky and a glimpse of St Paul's to the
south of it. It is a lovely work and so good *outside*, which is what matters
most. Osbert pointed out how shoddy it makes that dreary Hayward
Gallery look. Your theatre looks so good from so many angles, that I
think it will even survive horrific chests of open drawers or whatever
slabs they put up south of it. It has that inevitable and finished look
great work does. It is so river and wash scenery too and reminds me of a
sketch of the Thames ascribed to Rembrandt I saw somewhere.

(dotted lines
indicate
Seiferts!!)

Of course County Hall is not the way to build on the South Bank.
Your theatre shows it up. St Thomas's Hospital doesn't. Currie is better
there with his old hospital, though it is a bit repetitious.

Museums

SPECTATOR. 29 OCTOBER 1954

Going into the excellent and exciting Baroque exhibition in the Victoria and Albert, I could not help noticing that even there the museum policy of imagining we are all children and have to have notices in large letters to tell us what is what, prevails. There is a tendency here, though less, fortunately, than in other museums, only to show a few choice objects and to put everything else in the basement. I was talking to a high-up museum official this week who secretly sympathised with my personal preference for the sort of museum which is crowded with miscellaneous objects, some good and some bad, like an antique shop. The museums at Wells and Ilfracombe are ones after my own heart. Such places are accurately described in the beginning of Tennyson's *The Princess*:

> And on the tables every clime and age
> Jumbled together; celts and calumets,
> Claymore and snowshoe, toys in lava, fans
> Of sandal, amber, ancient rosaries,
> Laborious orient ivory sphere in sphere,
> The cursed Malayan crease, and battle-clubs
> From the isles of palm.

Alas! one of my favourite museums, the Parkes Museum in the Royal Sanitary Institute, Buckingham Palace Road, London, is at present closed. They are getting it ready for an exhibition of single-stack draining. But I hope the preparations for this will not disturb the exhibitions of 'The Life of the Bed Bug' and 'The History of the Water Closet', both illustrated with models, which have long been its features. I hope, too, that the interesting collection of bus tickets and cigarette packets which I have myself inserted into some cases I found empty and open in the gallery, will not be disturbed. When the old Geological Museum was in Piccadilly, I gave some pebbles and horse-chestnuts to an empty case there and labelled them 'The Betjeman Bequest'. I have often wondered whether they were moved to South Kensington.

The Wembley Tower

From the script of METRO-LAND, a television film
first shown on BBC 2 in February 1973

Beyond Neasden there was an unimportant
hamlet
Where for years the Metropolitan didn't
bother to stop. Wembley.
Slushy fields and grass farms
Then, out of the mist arose
Sir Edward Watkin's dream.
An Eiffel Tower for London.
(Sir Edward Watkin, Railway King, and Chairman
of the Line
Thousands, he thought, would pay to climb the
Tower
Which would be higher than the one in Paris.
He announced a competition – 500 guineas
for the best design
Never were such flights of Victorian fancy seen.
Civil engineers from Sweden and Thornton Heath,
Rochdale and Constantinople
entered designs.
Cast iron, concrete, glass, granite and steel
Lifts hydraulic and electric; a spiral steam
railway.
Theatres, chapels and sanatoria in the air.
In 1890 the lucky winner was announced
It had Turkish baths, Arcades of shops, and
Winter Gardens.
Designed by a firm of Scots with a London office
Stewart, McLaren and Dunn.
It was to be one hundred and fifty feet higher
Than the Eiffel Tower.
But when at last it reached above the trees,
And the first stage was opened to the crowds,
The crowds weren't there. They didn't want to
come.
Money ran out
The tower lingered on, resting and rusting
Until it was dismembered in 1907.

[174]

PARKS AND OTHER PLEASURES

HACKNEY EMPIRE
THEATRE OF VARIETIES

Horace Malcham
Architect
London

1.

2.

3.

Completed in 1901. After the war it became a TV studio and then a bingo hall.
On 9 December 1986 it reopened as a live light entertainment theatre.

The Cockney Amorist

Oh when my love, my darling,
   You've left me here alone,
I'll walk the streets of London
   Which once seemed all our own.

The vast suburban churches
   Together we have found:
The ones which smelt of gaslight
   The ones in incense drown'd;
I'll use them now for praying in
   And not for looking round.

No more the Hackney Empire
   Shall find us in its stalls
When on the limelit crooner
   The thankful curtain falls,
And soft electric lamplight
   Reveals the gilded walls.

I will not go to Finsbury Park
   The putting course to see
Nor cross the crowded High Road
   To Williamson's to tea,
For these and all the other things
   Were part of you and me.

I love you, oh my darling,
   And what I can't make out
Is why since you have left me
   I'm somehow still about.

Coldharbour, Isle of Dogs, 1936

The Isle of Dogs

SPECTATOR. 1 JUNE 1956

In the evening sunlight on Monday, I went to that least visited part of London, the Isle of Dogs. It's more than a square mile of docks, houses, shattered Victorian churches, no train sevice, no cinema, a bus service, and only approachable by swing bridges. The people on the Island are proud of it and don't like living anywhere else. Poplar people on the mainland don't like coming to live on the Island. It is a cut-off kingdom, the remotest thing you can find in London, and was very badly bombed in the War. Among the ruins three sights well worth the journey are to be seen. (1) Coldharbour, near Blackwall Basin, where some fine Georgian merchants' houses have the water washing up to their walls and where a public house looks over Blackwall reach. (2) Island Gardens on the southern tip of the Island, which commands the best view of Greenwich Hospital there is. Reflected in the water one sees the doomed Union Wharf beside the Hospital with its weather-boarded houses, Queen's House, and in the background the trees of Greenwich Park and the outline of the Observatory. (3) One of the best new housing estates I have seen since the war, comparable with Lansbury, intimately proportioned, cheerful and airy and yet London-like. It is called Castalia Square and makes one realise, when one compares it with the gloomy blocks of 'artisans' dwellings' of the mid-war and pre-1914 periods, how good modern architecture can be. In all the destruction I record in this column, it is a pleasure to be able to write about something newly built which makes one's heart rejoice.*

*The Isle of Dogs is no longer a cut-off kingdom; many businesses, including a daily newspaper, have moved there and there are interesting new housing developments. The Docklands light railway was opened in July 1987 and has a stop at Island Gardens. Coldharbour has changed, externally, very little. Castalia Square is now thirty years old and has not worn well.

Crystal Palace Park

SPECTATOR. 26 JULY 1957

The day these words appear in print will be the last in which you can put in an offer for the strange statues the LCC is selling in the Crystal Palace Park. I believe Osbert Lancaster has put in a bid for Father Thames, though how he will get this huge lump of stone down to Henley, where he lives, I cannot tell.

The statues stand amid willow herb, bindweed and ivy, and some of them are buried so deep that it is hard to see what they are. Cherubs' faces peep coyly through the undergrowth out to the roofs of Anerley and Penge. This melancholy garden contains survivals, I suppose, of the splendid ornamental terraces laid out here in 1854 by, it is said, Sir Charles Barry. It still has its atmosphere of dead silk-hatted prosperity. Not even the television mast rising on the hilltop destroys it.

The Crystal Palace Park, indeed, used to provide the most thrilling summer evenings I remember in London. At sunset one would get out at the Low Level Station and walk down to those lakes where prehistoric

monsters rear themselves enormous and black against the sky from the swampy undergrowth. They are still there – the brontosaurus, dinosaur and pterodactyl and many another peculiar beast, and the LCC has given up any policy of arranging rock gardens round their feet.

Then one would climb up to the Palace itself to watch the fireworks soar into the Surrey sky and see the crystal walls of the Palace turn from green to red as they reflected the Bengal Lights. One walked back over the echoing boards of the Palace itself while the organ played in the central transept where names like Beethoven, Balfe, Mozart and Spohr were blazoned round the roof. One would take a last look at the Courts of Art, the Alhambra with its aspidistras, the Medieval Court by Pugin and so out to the High Level Station, where the Southern Railway pulled one home by Lordship Lane and Honor Oak.

London Airport

SPECTATOR. 11 MAY 1956

I have found a new London pleasure, and that is going to London Airport and sitting on that roof-garden which has just been opened, smelling the cheroots of rich Belgians and South Americans as they stroll behind me and watching more of them being absorbed whey-faced by the great building from the airfield in front. And I venture to think that it *is* a great building, the best work so far of its architect Frederick Gibberd. For one's entry to London this way is smooth and, despite the Customs, welcoming, with its climax the Great Hall, by night as splendid with clusters of naked bulbs as the nave of Westminster Cathedral, by day splendidly proportioned and detailed. The subsequent hideous bus journey into London is an anticlimax indeed. The airport is an enormous machine. It sucks the passengers up gently sloping corridors to the Customs Hall. One can select passengers from the roof garden and restaurant as they leave the aeroplanes and decide which one one would like to see at closer quarters and guess what their luggage will be like. Then one walks round to the entrance hall and finds the door by which they will emerge from the Customs, shattered or triumphant. There are comfortable waiting enclosures by these doors, and one can see the luggage sliding out, crematorium fashion, from the Customs on a revolving band to the porters waiting on the ground floor. The doors open and here is the passenger going to join his luggage. Devoted as I am to railways, London Airport is more interesting even than Euston or St Pancras or beautiful, doomed Cannon Street.

London in August

SPECTATOR. 29 JULY 1955

As I am staying in London after Goodwood and not going to Cowes this year, nor even to my usual moor for the Twelfth (the children and their nanny being sent to lodgings in Frinton where their mother hopes to join them for a night), I shall be foot-free in London for most of August, and shall have to wander about with Jehovah's Witnesses who now seem to be crowding Piccadilly Circus and Leicester Square. But as a matter of fact I enjoy being in London in August more than at any other time of the year. What pleasure it is to join in municipal putting over the burnt grass in Finsbury Park! What joy too to rattle out in a half-empty suburban train to metro-land and what remains of the Green Belt, and in the evening walk from the station to hear the whirr of the lawn mower, the plop of the tennis ball and the anxious voices of mothers calling unwilling children from the garden depths to bed.

One Tree Hill

SPECTATOR. 28 JUNE 1957

Last week some friends took me to the nearest and strangest piece of country surviving in London. This was One Tree Hill, near Honor Oak Park, in South London. From its leafy height one could see St Paul's and the Houses of Parliament, a golf course, green levels and in the distance on a fine day Windsor and Epping. As a prospect it was better than that from Parliament Hill on Hampstead Heath. On one slope is a church, locked like so many in the Southwark diocese. On the other is a deserted garden. We walked through a gap in the fence through long grass to a plaster Gothic house called 'The Abbey'. The door was open, the carpets were on the stairs, a steel engraving of a scriptural subject had its glass smashed and the face of Our Lord dented in. From the empty rooms was a marvellous view over tree tops to St Paul's. The whole place seemed to be awaiting a terrible doom in the hot sunshine.

The Agapemonite Church

Delight in E5, Springfield Park

SPECTATOR. 6 APRIL 1956

Tempted by the sun I opened my London atlas and looked for a public park I had not yet seen. I know most London parks; clock golf on the heights of Finsbury; the dull extent of Queen's Park, NW, whose acres are covered with that arid soot-resisting grass beloved of the LCC; Golder's Hill with its gorgeous sweeps of cedar-shaded lawns looking across to the azure heights of Hendon; but fortune took me to Springfield Park on the east side of Clapton Common. Tall trees, a pond and a slope of crocus were in the foreground, on the left a stucco regency villa, with the usual forbidding municipal cafeteria, then a steep grass slope to the River Lea and beyond the huge lakes of East London's reservoirs with wooded islands on them and in the distance the range of Epping Forest. It was a vast sun-dappled view totally unexpected. I hired a boat on the Lea below and rowing in the filthy water past Peggotty-like constructions in a boat-yard on the Essex bank and the untamed flats of the Hackney Marshes, heard Great Eastern trains puffing emptily over viaducts to Chingford and Tottenham and saw the slender steeple of the Agapemonite church peering over the trees of Springfield Park.

South London Sketch, 1844

Lavender Sweep is drowned in Wandsworth,
   Drowned in jessamine up to the neck,
Beetles sway upon bending grass leaves
   Shoulder-level to Tooting Bec.
Rich as Middlesex, rich in signboards,
   Lie the lover-trod lanes between,
Red Man, Green Man, Horse and Waggoner,
   Elms and sycamores round a green.
Burst, good June, with a rush this morning,
   Bindweed weave me an emerald rope
Sun, shine bright on the blossoming trellises,
   June and lavender, bring me hope.

Summoned By Bells

And so, at sunset, off to Hampstead Heath
I went with pencil and with writing-pad
And stood tip-toe upon a little hill,
Awaiting inspiration from the sky.
'Look there's a poet!', people might exclaim
On footpaths near. The Muse inspired my pen:
The sunset tipped with gold St. Michael's church,
Sounds of boys bathing came from Highgate Ponds,
The elms that hid the houses of the great
Rustled with mystery, and dirt-grey sheep
Grazed in the foreground; but the lines of verse
Come out like parodies of A & M.
    The gap between my feelings and my skill
Was so immense, I wonder I went on.

Highgate Ponds

Index

[189]